HERE AND NOW

A Spirituality for the Redeemed

by

George R. Leonard

[handwritten: Peter Bonne Radlett 1993]

Hodder & Stoughton
LONDON SYDNEY AUCKLAND

Publisher's Note

Mgr George Leonard was able to complete this book before he died on 20 January 1993. Hodder and Stoughton are glad to publish it in his honour.

British Library Cataloguing in Publication Data

A catalogue record for this book is available from the British Library

ISBN 0-340-59735-6

First published in Great Britain 1993

Published by Hodder and Stoughton, a division of Hodder and Stoughton Ltd, Mill Road, Dunton Green, Sevenoaks, Kent TN13 2YA
Editorial Office: 47 Bedford Square, London WC1B 3DP

Typeset by Phoenix Typesetting, Ilkley, West Yorkshire.

Printed in Great Britain by Cox & Wyman Ltd, Reading, Berks.

Contents

To Rosetta, Christine and Lucia,

I remember to this day the desolation I felt after my father's death as I left the hospital in Warrington with a brown carrier bag containing all his personal effects. What was left of seventy-two years of struggle, dreams and devotion was neatly itemised, parcelled up and consigned to official oblivion. The image returns to haunt me. Possessions and enduring monuments play little or no part in the life of a priest. But an instinct for permanence remains. I want to show something for my life which is not at the mercy of fading memory and fragmentation. It has become very important for me to set down some of the ideas which now excite me and shape my responses to life. I feel committed to express in a variety of ways and in different contexts what I have authentically experienced. There is no master-plan behind these notes and reflections; they are only a kind of mirror which reflects my changing self as I try to make sense of my life and relate it to a deeper, lasting reality. You have walked the same pilgrim road with me over more than the three or four years mapped in these pages. I want to leave you this book because I think you understand and will not forget.

Foreword

One week before his sudden and unexpected death George Leonard handed the manuscript of this his first and only book to the publishers. He died not knowing whether or not it had been accepted for publication. For much of his life George had helped others to express their thoughts in books, articles and statements, hiding his own thinking and yet putting his skill with words at the disposal of those whom he was serving. I, in particular, was a beneficiary of this generosity. Nonetheless it had always been important to him, as he has written, 'to set down some of the ideas which . . . shape my responses to life'.

This book has the character of notes and reflections which are 'a kind of mirror which reflects my changing self as I try to make sense of my life and relate it to a deeper, lasting reality'.

It is his attempt to write about that 'deeper, lasting reality' which gives this book its special character and significance. Spirituality is never an easy subject for any writer. There are many books which tell us about how we should think and behave, and these have their own special value, but it is especially refreshing to read a book which seeks to explore God himself in so far as this is ever possible. It is good to be able to take our eyes off ourselves and to try to fix our gaze on God. How successful George has been I leave to the judgement of you, the reader. Note especially the last chapter of the book entitled 'Pentecost'. I have found this to be one of the best reflections on the coming of the Holy Spirit that I have ever read. I suspect that George wrote this last and it constitutes in a marvellous way his last testament.

In this book George tells us something of his struggle to free himself of the shackles of a false spirituality – one based on an unhealthy fear – and to discover the liberating joy of realising the power and intimacy of God's love for each one of us. George was very critical of the early training which he received at school and seminary and, with hindsight, one can see that such a training was too restrictive and inhibiting. On the other hand, for many of us that process was important as a stage through which we had to go in order to discover a freer and warmer response to God.

Responding to God's love is always demanding, sometimes painful. The spirituality outlined in this book is particularly attractive and invigorating, but it is no easy option. Furthermore, God's spiritual gifts are often preceded by periods of darkness and coldness. There are hints here and there in this book that George had experienced the dark night of the soul. This phenomenon is more common than we may think. It is God's way of preparing us for a greater understanding of who he is and what it is to know and to love him.

The central theme of this book is a call to a new heightened awareness of the reality of divine love ever-present at the centre of all creation. It is full of surprising connections between the everyday and the sacred, between science and theology. At the heart of this book is an exploration of what it means for God to have become man, and it sparkles with sharp and penetrating insights which help us to reflect on this central Christian truth.

I believe this to be an important book by a priest who served his Lord and Master well and in a manner that was generous and selfless, at the same time endearing himself to a great number of people. They will hear his voice coming through every page of this fresh and inspiring contribution to Catholic thought.

Basil Hume

NOW I SEE

Introduction

Many people experience a sense of unreality as they try to hang on to the Christian standards, customs and worship that shaped their lives in the past. Many Catholics of the older generation, and they are people I know very well, look around their personal landscape after the hurricane of change and renewal that was unleashed in the sixties by the Second Vatican Council. They find familiar landmarks swept away, old paths obliterated, signposts blown down. Like others, particularly in Western society, they live also in a prevailing atmosphere of unbelief and moral confusion.

Some have dug for themselves protective shelters of one kind or another. They occasionally lift their heads above the parapet, seeking a friendly face and wondering whether life as they once knew it will ever return. Others, to drown out siren voices, turn up the volume of their favourite programmes of religious comfort and teaching. They resort to simplicity, familiarity and fundamentalism. Yet others channel their religious energy into anger. They seem to regret that the winds of change have not swept the Church and the world clear of everything that existed before and now seems obsolete. They yearn intemperately and immediately for new heavens and a new earth. When the real Church and the real world remain stubbornly imperfect, they react with frustrated rage.

Part of the problem is located in the undeniable fact that many of us spend much of our lives looking for the wrong things from religion. We expect to find a formula that will bring us final security and lasting happiness. Instead we are offered personal and limitless potential. We would love to settle for the observance of regular ritual and some definite, and limited, moral code. We would like to depend on the Decalogue. But a lifetime of religious exploration has led me painfully to conclude that Jesus Christ did not come primarily to uphold law and order or to preach a sensible and balanced moral system but to call people out of themselves on a perilous pilgrimage of love.

There is in St Matthew's Gospel a vivid pen-picture of someone very like many of us. I call him 'the thirteenth apostle', a might-have-been man. The portrait loses nothing if you remember it purports to come from the pen of a reformed renegade, an evangelist who put behind him extortion and tax-gathering to follow his Master.

'And behold, one came up to him, saying, "Teacher, what good deed must I do, to have eternal life?" And he said to him, "Why do you ask me about what is good? One there is who is good. If you would enter life, keep the commandments." He said to him, "Which?" And Jesus said, "You shall not kill, You shall not commit adultery, You shall not steal, You shall not bear false witness, Honour your father and mother, and, You shall love your neighbour as yourself." The young man said to him, "All these I have observed; what do I still lack?" Jesus said to him, "If you would be perfect, go, sell what you possess, and give to the poor, and you will have treasure in heaven; and come, follow me." When the young man heard this he went away sorrowful; for he had great possessions' (Matt. 19:16–22).

This story records one of history's great lost opportunities. The young man was no moral weakling nor a reprobate. Quite obviously he was a person of sterling worth, clean-cut, responsible. He had grown up in a fiercely religious tradition and took his religious commitments with utter seriousness. He was a dutiful son, a loyal Jew, a sincere and compassionate man. Jesus loved him – Mark in his account is explicit on this point. He called him to follow him, to be the thirteenth apostle. The young man listened and realised that to follow meant to cut loose from security, to commit himself to a crazy adventure of love and faith. And he could not do it.

We are told simply that he went away sad because 'he

was a man of great wealth'. Perhaps he was weighed down by his obligations and the duties laid on him as a result of his wealth. There would be others who looked to him for employment, shelter, food. There would be members of the family who relied on his careful handling of the family resources. Whatever the reasons, he felt he could not risk all for the sake of the kingdom. Prudence, common sense, the pull of the past were all holding him back. And so the thirteenth apostle disappears from the pages of the Gospel. We never found out his name.

In our own lives we are constantly presented with the invitation to make brave choices, to leap into the uncertainties of the future with faith as our sole security. Decisive choice and courageous acceptance of consequences are as rare today as in the past. Without them we remain locked not in the spiritual childhood so beloved of Jesus Christ but in immaturity and frustration. True childhood is essentially transitional and is not an end in itself. It is a time of ceaseless development. When Christ said that the kingdom could be entered only by children he was opening our minds to the truth that his followers must be constantly on the move in search of fulfilment and the Promised Land.

Many people reach the plateau of middle-age psychologically long before they arrive there physically. Most studies of middle-age talk of the sense of flatness or of boredom. People seem to lose their zest. They settle down within the limits they have fixed for themselves. This attitude of the middle-aged is a trap about which Jesus warned us by his insistence on the importance of childhood. A Christian should never settle for anything less than constant growth. There are all sorts of philosophical and theological reasons why every individual should go on learning, loving and experiencing until the end. Attitudes are all-important. A sense of wonder and acceptance, an ability to be constantly surprised by oneself, by others and by life itself, an endless curiosity are the three best gifts that a fairy godmother can give to anyone.

My generation was brought up largely on self-doubt and a rather gloomy introversion. It is not surprising that few were encouraged to explore further the riches of spirituality. We are now more clearly aware that growth as a person consists essentially in laying to one side fears, anxieties and defence mechanisms. We need to develop self-esteem and sober respect for the goodness and abilities within us. As Andrew Greely once wrote: 'The greatest single obstacle to bringing good to others is the fear that we have no good to give.'

We are lucky enough to live in one of history's most dramatic periods of growth and discovery. It is an age to rank with the Renaissance or the birth of the Middle Ages. Christian belief needs a new Augustine, a new Thomas Aquinas to articulate what many now stammer to express. Just as urgently we need mystics and poets to explore the landscape of the spirit. What I have experienced and am struggling to communicate is not so much a self-assured discovery but more a first draft of a spirituality and an appeal for others to corroborate and advance it.

1: Towards a Single Vision

Only now am I coming to realise the depth and extent of the alienation I had always felt from my inner self, from others and from the world. Without question the religious formation I received in the years of childhood and adolescence and the values and attitudes I then embraced with such intensity helped to strengthen and give a kind of divine sanction to this sense of being different, detached and basically at odds with life. I know I am far from being alone in this. Those of us who survived Catholic education in the middle years of this century were constantly made aware of the rich heritage of the past but were very deliberately made conscious that we were for ever strangers and exiles in this vale of tears. Here we had no abiding city. Life was hazardous and full of menace. We tiptoed through a moral minefield, half-expecting at any moment and despite our best endeavours to find ourselves guilty of sin and worthy of everlasting damnation. For those of us who were imaginative, easily impressed, scrupulously conscientious, the flesh and the spirit were in constant conflict. The body continued to beckon seductively and insidiously. The only possible posture was felt to be one of constant watchfulness and extreme suspicion.

There is most probably in this picture some element of distortion, of heightened memories. My experience was that of a junior seminarian of those days, taken from parents, family and familiar surroundings in the immediate pre-adolescent years and brought up in an over-protected and ex-clusively male environment among others being remotely pre-pared for the rigours and demands of celibate priesthood. But in different ways this formation and these attitudes had been shaping generations of priests and religious and, inevitably, came to influence the spirituality and expectations of the Catholic community.

History too played its part. Whether we were Irish or English we were encouraged mightily to remember the past and to be proud of the faith of our fathers. The centuries of Irish suffering for national identity and for the Church made it certain that we would never identify with British imperialism or Protestantism. Those who traced descent from stubborn Recusant stock never forgot that they were the disinherited and true heirs to the cathedrals, parish churches and abbeys now in other hands. The faith was treasured as the pearl beyond price but it was to be received in un-questioning and humble simplicity and zealously guarded. It was in danger of contamination from alien ideas, influences and social pressures. The ghetto was the safest place for a religious and cultural minority to thrive in isolation. We instinctively adopted a siege mentality, intensely aware of the differences between us and them.

There was more. No matter how resolutely we refused to admit it, the image of God at the heart of our religious ex-perience owed much to our cultural, social and psychological expectations at that time. Certainly – and for years without any questioning – I clung to the assumption that there was a space beyond all imaginable space where God really was, that there was a time beyond time where God for eternity exists in total and blissful isolation. I tried without much success to relate this God up there and out there to the vivid, experi-enced reality of my here and now world. God's eyes watched us with loving but unwavering intent. His ears listened to our every prayer but were sometimes inexplicably deaf to our pleas. He was angered by our waywardness, pleased by our good actions. He watched over the world he had made and could be persuaded by our faith and unwearying prayer to intervene in events sometimes quite dramatically in order to ensure our safety, heal our sickness, secure our continuing health of mind and body and promote our good fortune. If he failed to do this, if disasters struck our world, faith was then put to the test. We could begin to doubt his very existence. God, despite all our protestations to the contrary, was widely seen as the puppet-master, as the playwright, producer and director of the human drama in which we were the principal players. Secretly we believed that the whole production was staged for our benefit and the plot arranged so that at the denouement we might save our souls and be allowed a happy ending. Crudely, nothing else mattered provided that I narrowly escaped condemnation and found my way to heaven, even if that were only after a purgatory that would painfully purify me from the stain of my sins and cleanse me for the presence of God.

It took years to break free from the grip of these images and misconceptions. I can now pinpoint the time and place when I finally realised, in what seemed a blinding moment of illumination but which was in reality the climax of a lengthy process, that this world is no mere antechamber to paradise nor our life simply a time of test and preparation for the life to come. I was driving home one night on a motorway of all places. Suddenly the sense of being alien was finally swept away. For the first time I felt utterly and absolutely at home in myself and my world. I came to realise with utter conviction that the billions of years which so far have shaped the cosmos and the four and a half million years of human growth and evolution are not an irrelevance but a process to secure the survival of our human family and to ensure that we are increasingly attuned to life on our home planet. This is the place we are meant to be. We are equipped to develop its potential and to harness its resources to new and ever more effective use. Our role as prophetically indicated in the Scriptures is to make real and conscious the presence of God in our world here and now. The womb from which we all sprang is the nurturing cosmos which is essentially and constantly sustaining and renewing. As modern jargon might describe it, the universe and all within it is by God's design 'user-friendly'. Inanimate creation and the animal kingdom fulfil God's purpose by the nature of their being. Humankind, in exercising choice, can be inadequately informed, selfishly motivated and subject to

many influences that can cloud the mind and warp the judgement. But the fundamental thrust of our energies has been
and will continue to be for the ultimate development of our
planet and the appropriate and positive use of its potential.
I know many would come to a more negative conclusion
but I have become convinced that through the human family
the purposes of God are being effectively pursued. This is
bound up intimately with an approach to spirituality which
has been slowly shaping up in my life over the past few years
and which can be seen as its unifying thread.

2: Setting Free

One day, quite distinctly, and quite late on in my life, I realised I was not scared any more. For the first time I was not haunted by fear of failure or the future. I did not feel like shying away from other people who might ignore, oppose or threaten me. I found it possible to like myself for the first time in my experience and to realise that what I was and had to offer had value. I realised that the pressures which drove me so relentlessly were really all inside me. Perhaps my experience might speak to others who began from where I began and help to free them too from a kind of slavery. Basically we are all on the same road; we dream the same dreams and experience the same tensions and failures. Like St Paul (Rom. 8:18–23) we long for the moment of rebirth. Creation groans in travail. We too groan inwardly as we wait for our bodies to be set free. Why is it that two thousand years after Christ the labour continues and freedom and spontaneity can seem as far away as ever?

Where to begin? My own liberation began from the dawning realisation that I did not need to earn love. It is not so much a feeling that God likes me or is pleased with me for my good works but rather a realisation that he can never stop loving me with absolute, unswerving love. His love in no way depends on my response. He has spoken his Word – it can never be taken back. That is why I exist. I embody a unique statement about God. I did not become that through my own efforts and achievements. And I am a single word, not divided. I live, and, in this unity, my body, my physical reality is not an afterthought nor an irrelevance. This body of mine – so often ignored or fiercely resented – is as much part of

God's loving regard as my immortal soul. It cannot be thought of except as integrated with my soul and destiny. So my body is to be loved, cherished, cared for, provided for, trusted. Its needs and its potential, its energies and its functions are essential to God's purposes: 'he loves every hair of our heads'. Our bodies are part of his plan for the world's healing and redemption. Christ made the blind see and the lame walk. He was not pointing a moral but reversing and restoring reality. The physical, the material, is also a word of God.

So I who am loved am free to love others. The same miracle of God's creation that made me also made all that is, and all that lives. I am in no sense independent nor can I exist for a moment except as part of a cosmic web of relationships. In looking at any other human beings, I must recognise and revere the reality of the Godhead which made them and which they embody. Seeing Christ in others is not an exercise of piety but a sober awareness that they too are God's Word, an expression of his truth, beauty and goodness.

All too often it is hard to discern the image of God in some of his sons and daughters. The reality never ceases to struggle into existence no matter how it is frustrated by sin, ignorance and sheer selfishness. But in all my human relationships I must never resent or deny, never seek to dominate or feel envy, always be free to reach out, love and sustain. Most times it is not easy or spontaneous. This is what it means to die to oneself and to live for God. That does not mean a fierce and violent doing to death of all one's instincts, needs and independence but instead is a surprised, loving, liberating experience. It means that I, as a word of God, have my being and my unique place in the midst of a magnificent and loving creation which echoes God and becomes a canticle of praise and thanksgiving to its creator and sustainer. I look at it all and take part in it with trust and love and a realisation that I am, in Alan Thornhill's phrase, 'a God-filled nobody'. I am nothing in myself, but immortal and invincible in the God who gives me life.

We must not make the mistake of narrowing down God's Word to our own capacity for knowing and loving nor confining it to the merely human and the personal. Liberation and enrichment come from understanding that God is the God of all creation. We see him not simply in the spectacular beauties of nature but in all that exists. Here and now he is to be found in all the living things around us, in all the energies and reality of our material world. All is sacred: the animals, birds of the air, fish of the seas, the plants, flowers, trees, crops and fruit, the cycles of the seasons – the evolving of our universe. God meant us to grasp this lesson and to see its secret significance when after revealing himself to us in flesh and blood he continued to be present in us and for us in bread and wine, 'which earth has given and human hands have made'. This planet and the billions of other worlds, in ways we do not yet comprehend, reveal his splendour and his love. We have to accept them all as part of our God-given trust even though we may seriously ask ourselves whether we are not still suffering from a serious 'small-town syndrome' in thinking that the sweep and magnificence of the unfolding cosmic story must necessarily have our planet and human family as its main characters.

For the present, however, I am convinced we can discover the glorious freedom of the children of God when we learn to see that all things, ourselves included, have no meaning apart from God. We are all his Word and Christ has opened our eyes to the true marvel of our humanity. We who are loved – who are part of this endless conspiracy of love – can do no other than rejoice, give thanks and revel in the free gift of God. But, and this too is significant, we are not simply passive spectators. We seem to be stunningly privileged since we are part of the process of that creating and share with God in the making of his universe. That is a task so absorbing and so significant that personal inadequacies and anxieties can be left to one side as irrelevant and irrational.

3: Our Response

Anyone who really troubles to look at us to see us for what we are, who regards us with the eyes of love, sees something of God in us. The more human we are, the more like God we are. We are strangers in our own home. We are flesh and blood, rooted in our world, yet we are stirred by dreams of long-lost grandeur. We yearn for new horizons and for an ecstasy beyond our mortal experience. Humankind is, to the best of our present knowledge, alone in the universe. We alone are able to understand, to reason, to plan, to reflect. We alone are free to reach out to choose, free to love and to relate to others. We walk the paths of this world like beggarmen who once were kings, but we are each of us an immortal. What is in us of God will never die. God's Word spoken in us can never fall silent. For better or worse we are destined to live without end. And that is part of our glory and part of our trial. It is our lasting joy; it could be our endless distress.

In the deepest heart of ourselves we realise that we are utterly unique. We are called out of nothing by God; called by our own name. God's everlasting purpose shaped us, placed us in this great design, holds us with fierce gentleness in the embrace of his love. We are each piercingly alone with God and with our destiny. For ever.

Yet, at the same time, we are made for friendship, partnership, fellowship and unity with others. While we are personally and fearfully responsible for ourselves, we also carry with us our brothers and sisters and we are carried in our turn by them. Each to the other is a precious burden, our own flesh and blood, humankind meant by God to be one family, one people.

We look back down the centuries and even at the dawn we recognise with delight the unmistakable faces of our brothers and sisters. In the firelight of the caves we can trace the outlines of beast and humankind drawn perhaps to celebrate the triumph of a hunt or to invoke the blessing of the gods. We know beyond doubt that our people were here, for as Chesterton once wrote: 'art is the signature of man'.

We walk through the silent circle of Stonehenge. We puzzle over its meaning but we recognise the work of our kith and kin. We stand in amazement before pyramids and temples, ancient amphitheatres or the petrified remains of Pompeii; we marvel at the delicacy of Oriental pottery, at the vibrant colour of medieval glass; we catch the tumbling words of Shakespeare, the music that captures the genius of the Germans. Through the ages, in every land, in tongues we fail to comprehend, we hear the voice of our people, the mind of humanity, the passion and the tenderness that are the mark of mankind.

We look at each other with a sense of wonder and companionship. We recognise a brother, a sister. We lift up our eyes and the eyes which look back into ours speak of family, tell of one father, tell us of Christ, our brother. Black or brown, yellow or white, the people of this global family are our flesh and blood, are Christ's flesh and blood.

I once came across an anonymous plea for pardon to God:

> O Lord, pardon me three sins.
> I have thought you – who are beyond thought.
> I have described you – who are indescribable.
> And in visiting temples I have forgotten
> that you are everywhere.

We who are of the West are temperamentally inclined to be pragmatic, aggressive and busy about many things. More than our forefathers, more than people from many other cultures, we divide and pigeonhole reality. We make arbitrary distinctions between religion and real life; we rigidly separate the things of God from the things of Caesar.

The great religions of the world have constantly encouraged

the search for holiness and wholeness. As Christians we have
a distinctive, in fact unique, approach. While other religions
in general attempt to spiritualise material reality, Christ
teaches us to accept the human, trace in human nature
the grand design of the creator and restore to its original
glory the humanity willed by God. This follows from the
basic insight of Christianity that God has taken flesh and
blood, become man and in so doing has transformed humanity and all human history.

Christians can never or, rather, should never ignore or
reject what is material, earthly and human. They should
try to restore it to its original grandeur when it came
mint-fresh from God's creating hand reflecting without distortion the mind of the creator.

As Catholics say every time they celebrate Mass: 'Heaven
and earth are full of your glory: hosanna in the highest.' Part
of our response to life is to stand in delight and awe before
God's creation; to offer thanks for what is given; to praise
its beauty and what it reflects.

We are not to stand idle in the marketplace because no one
has hired us. We must never separate our work, our industrial
life, our scientific, academic and creative labours from the
totality of our lives. We in fact adore and praise God in practical and inventive ways when we share God's creative action by
our labour and technical knowledge. We shape material things
to better advantage, harness natural energy for the benefit of
mankind or restore the ravages caused by adverse conditions
or by industrial pollution and commercial exploitation.

The world is from God. We need to accept it from his
hands as stewards. We have a special vocation in addition
towards human nature, our own and that of all the people
with whom we come into contact. Like the Jews before them,
Christians have always believed that human beings are made
in the image and likeness of God. Heart and mind reflect the
intelligence and love which is the very life of God. Pride and
disobedience broke the bonds of friendship between man
and his maker. Human nature then resembled a flawed masterpiece; the beauty was overlaid by new patterns, a reworking of

the original that obscured but never obliterated the primeval beauty.

Then the Jewish and the Christian understanding differ. The Christian sees in the person and life of Jesus a restoration, indeed a transfiguration, of human nature that can be detected in its full beauty only by the eye of faith. The Christian, unlike the Jew, believes that the power of God's love one day overshadowed a Jewish maiden and that the child born to her was the Holy One of God.

When the Word became flesh and dwelt among us the human race was offered a fresh start. A new Adam was born. His words, actions and the relationships he made established a way of being human that is instantly recognisable as human even if he transcends all known categories.

In him, mankind was shown the height and the depth, the breadth and the length of its own nature. It can now see what it means to be 'filled with the fullness of God' (Eph. 3:19). St Paul, with characteristic insight, said to the Christians of Ephesus: 'We are God's work of art, created in Jesus Christ to live the good life as from the beginning he had meant us to live it' (Eph. 2:10).

To reach that peak of divine love, we have constantly and clearly to focus our minds and hearts on the wonder of God. We need to explore the mystery of God. God is the spring of all life and all existence. God is the beating heart, the power of love at the centre of the universe, its origin and its sustainer. God the Infinite, God the Terrible, is all beauty, truth and power.

Men and women have always felt instinctively that sinful humans cannot look on the face of God and live. Adam and Eve after their rebellion against God hid themselves from him in the Garden of Eden. Primitive peoples have made unto themselves idols of stone, of silver and gold. Modern men, just as Chesterton observed, have refused to believe in God and so have come to believe in anything at all. Some believe in power or the party, in sex, in pleasure, in the purity of the race, in patriotism, some, God help us, even in market forces. Anything serves as a substitute for the

inescapable reality of God. The father of lies weaves endless
deceits.

Even those who profess faith in Jesus Christ often stop
short of an encounter with the living God. They are too fearful
to find themselves in that search for God which involves
purification and prayer. Instead they seek satisfaction and
a sense of security in a host of other worthy and 'churchy'
activities, which can be pursued with passion and absorption,
but which save them from the only thing which is necessary.

The list of substitutes is endless. They are good in themselves. They are praiseworthy indeed but the trouble is that
instead of being a means to the supreme end of union with
God, they are made into ends in themselves, and God is in
practice made redundant. People can become addicted to
hymn-singing, to liturgy, to church history, its traditions,
its architecture; they can become attached to this church
or that, this shrine or place of pilgrimage, this form of
devotion or that, this particular good cause, this political
objective or the other. All this is not only harmless but
positively enlivening, but only if our eyes are fixed always
and unwaveringly on God and our arms are outstretched to
embrace him and not some temporal substitute.

It is God, and God alone, who makes sense of the world
and of all human activity. It is God, and God alone, who
helps us give value and priority to human relationships and
not to material possessions. It is God, and God alone, who
explains us to ourselves, helps us solve our own mystery and
can lead us to fulfilment and that final, unending ecstasy.

Here are endless riches for us to plunder; even more profound depths for us to explore. God, the three-in-one, the
eternal and loving relationship of Father, Son and Holy Spirit,
is not remote, not forbidding. He has relevance, significance
and intimacy for our own lives. The mystery of the Trinity
beckons us inwards, into God himself but also into our inmost
selves. It is the precious centre of all Christ's teaching.

The Christian faith is not primarily about decency and
moral standards. It is not just about Church membership.
It is about a world reborn and a humanity recreated in the

image of Christ himself, Christ the Son, Christ the redeemer and reconciliator, Christ the risen and eternal. By faith in him, by baptism, through the one bread and one cup of the eucharist we are made one with Christ. We become other Christs. We are members of the body of Christ, and are alive now with the life of Christ.

And so we are identified with Christ, true man, true God. We are united with the Word of God who contains within himself the whole beauty, the entire truth and very nature of God the Father. The Father looks on the Son, and on us who are one with him, and loves him and us with endless, overflowing love. The Son, and we with him, looks to the Father, knows him with blinding clarity, utter truth – and loves him with an infinite love. The knowledge and love which exist between them, flow endlessly between them and overflow from them in the Holy Spirit. But what we hold beyond question is that we are part of it all. What we are unable to comprehend with our finite intelligence, what we cannot focus into words, what we cannot embrace totally with our hearts and wills, is still the reality of God in which we share, for in him we live and move and have our being.

We will and we must learn more, and experience more, in prayer and rapt contemplation. This is the end of all our striving, the yes to all our questions, the vision which inspires us, the goal of all our longings.

The words of Paul echo in our ears:
'Now this Lord is the Spirit and where the Spirit of God is, there is freedom. And we with our unveiled faces reflecting like mirrors the brightness of the Lord, all grow brighter and brighter as we are turned into the image that we reflect; this is the work of the Lord who is Spirit' (2 Cor. 3:18).

4: God and Us

All of us look in confused and different ways for the secret that
will bring us happiness. We seek the answer to our questions
and our doubts. We need something to give meaning to our
lives and rescue us from fear of failure, pain and ultimately
death. Even in a world supposedly as scientific and sophisti-
cated as ours, the search goes on. People scramble for security
and a sense of purpose in the pursuit of power, possessions
or pleasure. Or they seek some ease for their restlessness and
frustration in the sects, in the occult or in drugs. Ideally,
committed Christians should be able to come to church and
profess their belief in Jesus Christ. The Christian faith ought
to offer the only sure light in the darkness, a vision of hope,
resurrection and new life. Ideally, whenever we turn to God
in prayer or are aware of his presence in our lives, we should
realise that there is a meaning and a purpose behind everything
that happens, a plan of infinite subtlety and endless love.
Ideally, week by week, year by year, if we stay lovingly
faithful, the veil should lift that little bit more, we should
be led a little more deeply into the mystery of life and into
the wonders of God. Ideally it should be in the celebration of
the eucharist that Christians above all encounter the living God
– the God of all creation. The Church exists to lead us to God,
to unite us in God; anything less is counterfeit and fraudulent.
Yet it usually is not like that at all. Much of our public worship
is formal, superficial, ineffective. Religion is all too often
a cloak for unacknowledged inner violence and alienation.

A principal cause of inner emptiness in our own worship
is because our image of God is so often puny and child-
ish. Surprisingly we seem to care little about the constant

exploration of the mystery which is God. We prefer to bypass the marvel of the triune God. We make do with a familiar and by now threadbare concept of God. It may have been with us, essentially unchanged, since childhood. Most Christians take the Trinity, literally, on faith; we believe it, we profess it, but it means almost nothing to us as a source of energy and action. It is just there – like Mount Everest, the monarchy, mother love and apple pie. It remains part of our mental world, barely thought of from one year's end to the next, largely irrelevant to the real business of living. This is a tragedy, because it is really the heart of our whole existence, the key to the rest. Perhaps this is why we so often do not pursue more eagerly and thoroughly the vision which the Faith can provide. We do not hunger and thirst for God and the things of God. We fail to appreciate the treasures in our hands.

The prophet Joel once proclaimed: 'This is what I will do in the last days, God says: I will pour out my spirit on everyone; your sons and daughters will proclaim my message, your young men will see visions and your old men dream dreams.' At Pentecost so long ago in Jerusalem the final epoch of all history was inaugurated – the end-time – in which God who reconciled man to himself now offers this Jesus-life to all men and women, to every living soul, at all times, in all places through the active presence of the Holy Spirit. The Holy Spirit, by whose power Mary conceived and gave birth to Jesus, now overshadows the whole of humanity, all human life, and is engaged endlessly in a new and perpetual outpouring of creation. God is revealed as love-sick for man. The prophecy of Joel is fulfilled. The Trinity, the Godhead, is shown to be irrevocably committed to searching out the whole human family in order to envelop us, remake us and bring us into the heart of divine life and love through the Holy Spirit and in Christ.

The Trinity is not a closed circuit of love as if Father, Son and Holy Spirit were loving and being loved, knowing and being known in celestial abstraction and isolation. Instead the Trinity is for us. The Good News, the incredible news, is that the God who created the whole universe and supremely mankind itself in the image of his Son, the Word, and who loves creation endlessly and unconditionally in the Holy Spirit, sent his Son into the world after mankind had sinned and sought its independence from God. The Son broke the power of sin and shattered the slavery of humankind to evil. He manifested in his own self the harmony and reconciliation now effected between the divine and the human. Then, through the descent of the Spirit, God has founded a new people, a new Israel, a new temple in which Father, Son and Spirit will live for ever. The life of God is irrevocably given to a new community of believers.

We could perhaps be inclined to say that God has invaded the world of darkness and death, has established a beachhead, a footing on planet Earth and yet that language is itself deceptive. For God was never for a single instant driven out of his creation even by the rebellion of those made in his image and likeness. God never ceases to be everything in everything. We should be talking here instead of the conscious reawakening of humanity to his never-failing presence. The process of winning over men and women to God through Christ in the Spirit has begun. By virtue of this decisive, divine breakthrough in our history, any human being can become, through the Spirit, in the Spirit, a member of the family of God. 'See what love the Father has given us that we should be called the children of God; and so we are.'

So things are no longer what they seem to the non-believer, the materialist. The revelation of the triune God is a challenge. If it is true, and this is the only question that really matters, then our whole view of the world and of life becomes something almost unbearably exciting. If it is true, if God the Father wishes us to be a new creation, a new humanity consciously aware of the infinite life and love of the Spirit, then despite appearances, ordinary men and women are not mere flesh and blood, not doomed to decay and die. We are made immortal. We are restless for the infinite. Our hearts and also our minds cannot be satisfied till they both know and love the God who is three-in-one. It was for this we have been remade.

We become conscious too of our human solidarity. We are one body, a single unity with our kinsfolk, the men and women of our race who also carry within them the divine spark, the divine imprint. The Christian understanding and vision of God has major consequences for our Christian spirituality. The God revealed by Jesus Christ and in Jesus Christ, the Christian God, is instantly recognisable and is quite unlike the God of other faiths. The God of Jesus Christ must inevitably lead us into the world and not away from it. God did not become incarnate so that we might aspire to become disincarnate. A true Christian comes slowly to realise that all is holy and all is a single sanctified reality because all is made by the Father in the likeness of the Son through the love of the Spirit. God in Christ leads us into deeper involvement with life, not into condescension and a patronising rejection of the human.

The goal of many Eastern religions is to transcend the world and arrive at a godless nothing. Such a spirituality leads to the dissolution of the human individuality, the 'I' and indeed the whole world into Nirvana. Christian spirituality, by contrast, leads believers to discover and treasure the world and each individual life in God. As Fr John O'Donnell remarks: 'Christian spirituality is the mysticism of the world' (*The Month*, April 1989). Yet all too often in the past, Christian spiritual writers have tried to persuade us – with patchy results – to despise the world. They have talked about the pilgrimage of faith as a journey beyond the world towards the One God who has nothing to do with flesh and blood, with our human history, with our suffering, our loves, our dreams. Too often – and to our cost – the ideal of Christian holiness has been proposed as a flight from this world. Yet the goal of the Christian faith is not to transcend the world but to transform it. In our search for God we do not have to leave behind the world and all we love. All are destined for God's kingdom; all are destined for the resurrection. God is not the great Alone, but is a communion of love; he destines the world to communion. The world and all within it will not be lost or discarded but God will be all in all (1 Cor. 15:28). Our whole world-picture is relevant to the mystery of the Trinity.

But to think intensely about the Trinity leads us also into new self-knowledge and a new understanding of ourselves and our relationships. There is nothing Christian or spiritual in being consumed with self-doubt, or anxiety, or guilt, or self-disgust. There is now no unbridgeable chasm between the divine and the human. God is not outside our world, up there, out there, looking in, alien to our world, serenely different. The Spirit of God brought to birth in a Jewish maiden a human son who was also the Son of God, the second person of this Trinity God. That staggering and awesome claim – so faintly and inadequately believed by us even today – means that the human and the divine can never again be separate. The great ignored truth is that we are each of us reborn in the Spirit to be utterly identified with that Son of God. We are made one in Christ through the Spirit; in the Spirit we are loved without limit by the Father; in us – in all our frailty and limitation – he sees his Son and with us shares his life and love. As St Augustine said – and it can still shock and stun us – 'God becomes man so that man may become God.' We were never really taught that when I was young. We were kept on our knees, scourged with guilt, taught to despise our very humanity, to be, at best, on guard against others and our inmost selves, instead of being free and joyous in our new humanity and at peace with the family of God. It will take generations to repair the damage. We carry within us the wounded child and are in urgent need of healing.

5: Forgiven

One summer Sunday the liturgy of the Word at Mass retells the story of David's sin in taking the wife of Uriah the Hittite and of his repentance; it couples it with the story of Mary Magdalene and the washing of Christ's feet with her tears of sorrow. Both passages and their linking have over the years assumed great significance for me.

King David and Mary Magdalene leap out from the pages of the Bible as larger-than-life characters. They lived and loved extravagantly; they paid little or no attention to convention or to other people's opinion; they were capable of towering passion and intense repentance. They would make highly unusual pillars of any parish, and unlikely candidates today for priesthood and the religious life. That says as much about us as about them, but no matter. The point is that David's adultery, murder and remorse, Magdalene's harlotry, her tender and passionate repentance, are necessary reminders of some basic truths about ourselves, the way we live, how we relate to God and each other.

We seem to find it nearly always necessary to justify ourselves, to prove we are in the right, to claim credit for our efforts and actions. And yet, in truth, many of us take too little responsibility for our actions. When things go wrong we are like children caught in mischief: 'It wasn't me. It wasn't my fault. It just broke in my hand.' We make excuses. We blame others or circumstances. We lack moral maturity. It is a strange perversity of human nature that we can combine a miserably poor image of ourselves, a constant and depressing sense of guilt and inadequacy, with a pathetic touchiness and a feeling that our personal worth and merit deserve better recognition and reward from God and from others. Despite our protestations of humility and even in the very pursuit of perfection we can still be obsessively self-centred and fail to understand that Jesus Christ never asked us to go down that road. He decisively rejected any suggestion that we can find God and please him by our own efforts, our good works, our moral integrity. The scrupulous observance of rule, regulation and precept can be for some a psychological necessity. Of itself, however, it constitutes no more than the justice of the Scribe and the Pharisee; it is not the narrow way, the way of life. The Gospel demands that we relinquish any suggestion that we can redeem ourselves. We owe it all to the God who made us and to the Christ who saves us.

In all Christ's encounters with broken human lives he never stopped to subject them to recriminations or moral assessment before reacting. He never gave the slightest impression that he was deterred or disturbed by anyone's past life or depravity. Instead he was immediately moved by the depths of their distress. All he needed was a cry of pain, a plea for healing, a glimmer of trust and faith. His response then was simple and always the same. Your Father loves you, your sins are forgiven, now do the same for anyone who has harmed or wronged you. It could not be clearer or more emphatic. We are to live in the sunlight of God's unvarying love. It is much more than wiping the slate clean, giving someone a fresh start but under the same rules. It is a completely new ball-game where no celestial umpire keeps implacable score. It is a new experience of boundless, unconditional love. God our Father does not condemn. We, however, remain free to choose not to live and love. Death or life, denial or affirmation depend on our mature decisions, our free choice among the options in life. God calls us to commitment, responsibility, coherence as we learn to accept and make our own the Yes which is Jesus Christ. It involves us in growth as we relate intimately and, yes, passionately to the person of Jesus Christ and to all those in whom he still lives and moves and has his being. This is far removed from the attitudes and expectations with which I grew up and which I suspect are still those of most Catholics.

We were concerned largely with avoiding mortal sin and little with the life of the Spirit, with growth in love, with the coming of the kingdom, and making real the redemption.

The teaching of Scripture is directly relevant to our happiness, to our sense of guilt and personal failure. We are not under a cloud, nor are we on trial to see if we are worth saving. God has forgiven us and made us his own. If we do not have to justify ourselves, there is no need for us to eye others with suspicion, hostility or contempt. We can rejoice that we are saved by Christ, enjoy endless access to his life and love. We can be part of a people equally loved, precious and forgiven. We are a new creation, a people redeemed. That is reason for constant thanksgiving.

6: That I May See

Bartimaeus, the blind beggar of Jericho, is a Gospel character who has caught Christian imagination over the centuries. The Jesus Prayer is basically his. Picture the scene in your mind. A large crowd is noisily escorting Jesus out of Jericho. He is accompanied by his disciples. Squatting beside the dusty road, pitifully holding out his begging bowl, sits Bartimaeus. He must have heard of the wonder-worker from Nazareth, and when the crowd and the clamour draw near, he begins to cry out 'Son of David, Jesus, have pity on me.' He must have caused quite a commotion because they turn angrily on him and tell him to be quiet. That only serves to incite him to louder, more insistent cries: 'Son of David have pity on me.' Jesus hears him above the noise of the crowd and calls the beggar to him. 'Courage,' they say, 'get up, he is calling you.' Leaping to his feet he casts aside his cloak and comes to Jesus who says, 'What do you want me to do for you?' 'Rabbuni,' (Master), 'let me see again.' Jesus says: 'Go, your faith has saved you.' Immediately his sight returns and he follows Jesus down the road.

As we let the details of that much-loved story take hold of our imaginations we can focus on what Christians have seen in it down the centuries. Most interpret it as the awakening of the believer to life in the Spirit. Blindness – with its attendant handicap, darkness, confusion, helplessness – is taken in the Bible to represent our state as fallen and wayward human beings. Faith and hope are able to sense the significance of a chance encounter with Christ and to seize hold of it. Bartimaeus refuses to be restrained or deterred by anyone or anything that holds him back from Jesus. He makes it noisily clear that he is in dire need. When summoned to come to Christ he lets neither shame nor handicap deflect him. He wants only one thing. To see. Again, significantly, Christ makes physical healing a secondary, relatively unimportant aspect of a deeper healing. 'Go, your faith has saved you.' Restored to wholeness, saved, forgiven, his sight returns because the whole man is healed. He is free to move, to resume his independence. He chooses instead to follow Christ down the road, the way which always stands for progress in God and towards God.

'Lord, let me see again.' Meister Eckhart described the spiritual life as coming to see: awakening to the beauty, the truth, the unity which is God. Is it not significant that when we understand we say: 'Oh, I see'? We describe the highest exercise of our minds in terms of vision, insight, enlightenment. To know, to love: this is essentially the life of the spirit, the way we most closely resemble the God in whose image we are made. The pleading of Bartimaeus for his sight and his humble recognition of his utter need are echoes of our human yearning. We are called to be divine; we are to be true to the image of God which constitutes our deepest selves. Deprived of that we cry out, not in despair but in longing. We refuse to be satisfied until we know, until we can see. So much of our human distress is caused by disorder, blindness, hunger for that union with God from which perversely we also flee. We cannot love and act with justice and charity unless we first know.

We can be happy when like Bartimaeus our eyes are opened and we can make sense of our surroundings. It is crucial to our faith that we also seek understanding. We cannot be content to let ourselves fumble within the confines of our blindness. I have grown to be wary of those who praise 'simple faith'. I suspect they may duck the challenge and the perils of seeking to understand. Faith seeks understanding just as understanding has in the final analysis to give way to faith which is the ultimate leap of the mind into the depths of God's own understanding of himself.

The blind beggar who now can see walks the way with Christ. He can take in the countryside, see the faces of his fellow-pilgrims and learn from the passing scene. But his eyes never stray from Jesus. In the depths of his being he knows that he sees only by the light Christ has given him.

We too should never flinch from the need to see and understand, from the demands of our adoption as children of God. The whole of creation reflects the mind of God. Seeking understanding plunges us ever more deeply into the mystery that is God. Nothing human is alien to us as children of God. Everything on earth as in the heavens, in the billions of galaxies, reveals the glory and wonder of God. All is created out of love, to be savoured and enjoyed; we too celebrate, give thanks and like Bartimaeus should follow rejoicing down the road. This leads us into the prayer of silence and contemplation, which is not the privilege of the mystic but open to us all. We must be brave enough to become still and not to hide behind words, images and music. When we have learned to be mute and welcoming, when we constantly attend on the Lord in silence and expectancy, a new and captivating beauty is brought to birth within us. It is best experienced in times of prayer but the Spirit can suddenly and in many different situations seize the mind, the imagination, the creative energy of the one who listens. The committed, prayerful Christian explores the mystery in contemplation, the artist in the intensity of his or her art. There is also undoubtedly what I would describe as secular prayer, an intense communion with a sometimes unknown God. Theatre, music, the performing and the creative arts can be part of the rapture of Bartimaeus who once was blind but now can see and is dying to share.

There is in everyone a Bartimaeus yearning to see, to live to the full, to be free of all that denies or destroys sight. God is within, waiting to be released. We must never despise or condemn ourselves, nor others, to sterility and frustration. We bear a heavy responsibility if we fail to teach the ways of prayer, if we ignore the authentic spirit of artistic creativity.

Whatever we truly experience of the Spirit of God is the common heritage of all and should be shared. We need to give each other courage to walk boldly into the light and dare to see.

7: The Presence of Eternity

I find the stories of raising the dead to life in the Gospels strange and disturbing. They seem to belong to a bygone age. Despite Christ's promise that his followers would work even greater miracles than he and despite the continuing evidence of miraculous physical healing in Christian times and down to our own days, the dead today still remain emphatically dead. I cannot recall any well-authenticated miracle of raising the dead to life after the time of Christ and his apostles. Perhaps the reason is that miracles are not merely wonders but signs that point beyond themselves to eternal truths. Perhaps it is that after the rising of Christ from the tomb, the Easter miracle and sign, which is the unique witness, is already in place. His resurrection and the Pentecost re-creation of all existence mean that for believers the barriers between life and death have now crumbled. Already we possess eternal life and are so much part of God's life and love in Christ that here and now we are immortal, can never die and are for all time part of God's ceaseless life and activity. So for us, in the new age, it cannot be that widows' sons have to be restored again and again to their mothers since believers in Christ are now all beyond the power of physical death. Once Christ rose from the dead and lives, it changes completely how a believer in him relates both to life and death. It alters our perspectives and priorities. In one sense, we are all the widow's child and are raised already. We no longer are confined to the brutally short and painful limits of a fitful human existence. But there is this difference: the widow's son rose to die again; we are raised and never again taste death. What is now open to us is the prospect of immortality, of divine life, of abiding presence.

Will we come to the end of our physical lives? Of course, inevitably. Will we ever come back to be part of the human story on this planet? No, we have but a single experience to be cherished and used to the utmost. In what sense, then, is death conquered? How are we to be sure that our risen life in Christ is for evermore? What do the signs mean for us?

I think they are pointing us to consider more deeply what it means to be fully human and fully alive. The whole of God's revelation is meant to make us realise the wonder of our being. It has to be interpreted in light of what we discover about the origins of our universe and our planet. There came that awesome moment, perhaps no more than four million years ago, when, after 15 billion years of creative formation, human consciousness, self-awareness, the power to understand, the power to love, first made its appearance on our planet. This may be, or may not be, the unique presence of intelligent life in our universe, but for us humans it has meant that the life of the spirit became a reality. A power, transcending physical limitations of time and space, an energy that is timeless and without measurable shape or bulk, entered our world. But why? The religious experience of the Jewish people and the unique teaching and witness of Christ identify this spirit as made in the image and likeness of God. When intelligent, recognisably human life appeared on earth, a divine force and presence were made manifest. It has gradually to enter into ever fuller self-consciousness despite human blindness and self-centredness. That is the story of human progress, of light wrestling with darkness, with our as-yet-uncertain, partial knowledge and wayward love.

Jesus Christ opened our eyes to further, undreamed-of, horizons. Not only are we made like unto God, we are truly his sons and daughters. The human family is called to become identified with Christ, to be loved, by the Father through the Holy Spirit. With the incarnate Son we are to be continually made part of the physical universe, to renew the face of the earth, to recognise and realise the harmonies, the patterns of the whole universe, to bring creation to its fulfilment. That is our mission and our meaning. The human spirit does not disintegrate and grow old as our physical bodies disintegrate and grow old. We are for ever part of God's presence in his creation. That is partly what we mean by the communion of saints, namely, that the living and the dead are never to be separated and what has been human remains so for ever. We do not know how we are to remain aware of our identity after death and what form our immortal existence is to take. But like the risen Christ we are to be always there, always involved, always part of God's presence in the cosmos he has made and will always sustain. It is the power and presence of the spirit that gives life and reality. We are participants and sharers of that spirit here and now and for always.

A LIFE WE SHARE

Introduction

Few wake up on Sunday mornings with a tingle of excitement because today they are to go to church and to worship with fellow-believers. Very few expect ever in the course of one hour to be suddenly overwhelmed by the power and wonder of God and experience the ecstasy of his presence. Instead we expect familiar words, routine responses. For most of the time we are largely passive spectators at a ritual that is all too predictable. We have tamed God, placed controls on the channels along which his energy and inspiration travel and succeeded in turning God into a yawn.

It is little wonder that congregations are departing in droves. Someone remarked recently: 'We were promised the Kingdom of Heaven; we were given the churches.' We have become respectable, unremarkable, eminently safe and sane, expected to be staunch defenders of the status quo. Whatever binds us together as the contemporary Church seems to bear little relation to that firestorm of spiritual energy and power in the upper room where the Church came into being.

In the Bible there are three dramatic descriptions of the transforming power of God's Spirit. The first is the image of the Spirit of God brooding over the waters of chaos, bringing forth the universe in all its beauty and goodness and breathing into the dust of the earth, giving life to the first man. The second is when the Spirit of God came upon the virgin betrothed to Joseph so that of her was born he who was truly the Son of God. In that incarnation humanity was seized by the Holy Spirit and God became man. The third instance was when the power of the Spirit was poured out over the huddled followers of Christ to give new shape to community, to bring into being the body of Christ which was humanity restored, healed and lifted to dizzying heights.

Each of these three moments was decisive for our world. Each has consequences for the way we live and the understanding we have of ourselves. Each can be grasped only by faith.

For us, then, the single most important thing in our lives is our rebirth by baptism into the Church which is the body of Christ. It is well-nigh impossible for those of us baptised in infancy to capture in any vivid or imaginative way the wonder of that rebirth just as most of us are sublimely indifferent to the miracle of our natural birth. But we can more consciously become aware of the communion and shared life which are the Church. That is best experienced when we come in faith to that most secret and yet most public of divine mysteries, the Mass. There God comes among us in sign and symbol. There we are bound together in Christ and lifted up to the Father in a single sublime sacrifice of love and self-giving. There we eat and drink and are ever more deeply and vitally transformed into the living Christ. Through the reality of the Church we are truly in God and God is in us. In Christ we are loved without reserve by God who loved us first without any worth on our part. And we are sent out from the Mass into a broken world to bring healing, hope and a love which is never ours but is the Spirit of God living and loving through us.

People are searching without understanding for a faith to live by, a hope to sustain and a fellowship to give them support, warmth, the sense of being wanted and worthwhile. They are frequently deluded by secular substitutes. They fail to find satisfaction in the Church which seems so distant from the promise and bright morning of Pentecost. If only we were able to believe what we profess and did what we promise, the Spirit of God would find ways to lay down through us foundations for the kingdom of love, justice, peace and fellowship. In and through the Church the Spirit of God seeks constantly to renew the face of the earth.

1: The Fire of Love

Relentlessly the media pump out images of achievement and success. The creation of wealth and financial prosperity has become the supreme value. Compassion is caricatured and dismissed. The subtly varied and enthralling world of beauty, grace, humanity has been replaced by a market; artists, craftsmen, farmers, ordinary flesh and blood people and gentlefolk have been superseded by hard-eyed, frenetic devotees of the VDUs, acolytes of the exchange rates, rewarded by soaring salaries and the doubtful status symbol of a BMW. I wonder what upwardly mobile young professionals will do when they eventually find that their ladders are propped up against a collapsing system, a house of cards. Can Midas find the heart to renounce his fatal gift before he loses for ever his even more precious humanity?

The Pentecost experience is intensely relevant. Its symbols of wind, tempest and fire are images of destruction but also of purification, power and the release of elemental energy. Because I used not to think too deeply about my faith and the meaning of God in my world and life, I tended to think of all I read in the Scripture as relating to a world long dead, an almost make-believe world of wonders and marvels, of lovely legends far away from the harsh realities of my daily life in today's city. Yet the Bible is not fairyland. Here I read the secrets of the real world. God shares with me a vision of the truth, about the panorama of creation, about what is and will be. Scripture tells about the *making* of the world in goodness and love, and its *unmaking* through human pride and sin and destructiveness and about its *remaking* through obedience and suffering, love and exaltation. And the point I missed so often and so sadly for my own human growth is that all this is not remote and in the past, but is the hidden heart of present-day experience. The Fall is *now* and always. The Incarnation is *now* and always. The Redemption is *now* and always. Pentecost is *now* and always. The whole drama of the human race is ever present. Whether we like it or not, whether we realise it or not, we are part in our day of the greatest story ever told.

What then does Pentecost, the coming of the Holy Spirit, mean here and now? It marks the decisive re-entry, the irrevocable presence of God in our world. It is the fashioning of the age of the Church – when Christ is coming to be sacramentally and mystically in our world. He is constantly coming to live and work in and through us for the remaking of our world. It is immensely important to focus on one single aspect which is literally overwhelming. What does it really mean when God's love is let loose in my world and in me?

Lots of Christians at this point might shrug their shoulders and dismiss the thought as commonplace. We live all our life imagining we know that God loves us. We are familiar with the Christian vocabulary of love, the well-worn, no longer exciting images, the cosy, predictable world of the living and partly living. The plain truth is that the reality of God's loving, properly understood, shrivels up the ego with all its pretensions, and bursts out in new forms of life and love. It is a remake of reality, new heavens and a new earth; it births a new humanity which bears the marks of Christ, and is Christ.

In the perpetual Pentecost, the baptised, the believers, are made other Christs by the creative energy of the Holy Spirit, the power of God himself. Like Christ we are made the beloved of the Father in whom he is well pleased. I try, usually without success, really to grasp what it means to be loved by God – who literally *is* love. I try to imagine something of the immensity of God, of his awesome power and endless being. I think of what he has made and is making: the universe may well be 20 billion years old, our planet four and a half billion years old, human beings some four million years. Our lovely, incredible planet is just one of the nine planets orbiting the sun, which is our nearest star, but which is one of 100,000 million stars in our galaxy and that only part of an expanding universe made up of more than 100 billion galaxies. All of this is being made by God in a staggering, unbelievable outpouring of energy, life and love. The God who made all this loves me. The power that sustains all this cares for me with utter and absolute love. When God loves, he has to love with all his being. That love which animates, sustains, gives life and meaning to the universe and to me is the Holy Spirit. Small wonder that his presence is imaged in storm, tempest, blazing fire. There is nothing domesticated and conditional here. Love at this intensity and with this power is overwhelming energy. It intends to take hold of us and pour itself out through us on others and the rest of our world. That is why our Christian calling is not just a passport to a future heaven. Our human story is not being told so that I might scrape through one day into a personal and private happiness. Our Christian calling is a commitment to this same divine love, an acceptance into ourselves of this power, a readiness to bear this love to others. That is a demanding and all-consuming passion, in which self and self-interest have eventually to shrivel and die.

Some argue from the scale of the known universe to a rejection of any kind of special significance for our planet and our human family. We are simply dwarfed and rendered absurd. Certainly perspectives change when we accept imaginatively and creatively our limited place in the total scheme of things. It can be a liberation to recognise that the centre of the universe is elsewhere.

A similar transformation takes place when individuals discover the ability to accept the reality of themselves in relation to others. If we are no longer the centre around which all else revolves we are free to accept the truth and live it.

2: Our Humanity

They used to say of a certain politician that 'deep down, he's shallow'. It is a damning indictment but then it is meant to be just that. Often enough, however, we would have to admit of ourselves that we too, deep down, are shallow. We are creatures of moods, subject to short-lived enthusiasms and the urge to please and be accepted. We are so often distracted. We fail to grow and remain superficial. We lurch from one little crisis to the next, or are blandly unaware that there is ever a crisis. We wonder sometimes what sort of person we shall be when we grow up.

Do we ever have the ambition to be a deeply religious person? And if not, why not? Is it because, deep down, we do not make religion and the search for God the number one priority in life? And if not, why not? I have the hazy notion sometimes that many of us in reciting so blandly the Creed skate over the first few lines – 'We believe in one God, the Father, the Almighty, maker of heaven and earth, of all that is, seen and unseen.' Yes, we can take that for granted and only begin to register when we say 'We believe in one Lord Jesus Christ.' But if our awareness of God is limited and distorted, if our image of him subconsciously is infantile and unformed, then our understanding of Christ is rootless, inadequate. Is it too unkind to ask ourselves if we really believe in God? If we do, then do we shape our lives by that belief? Are we truly religious people? Am I, even as a priest, truly a believer?

It was Christopher Dawson who once said: 'Religion has its origins in the depths of the soul, and it can be understood only by those who are prepared to take the plunge.' There is no concession here to our comfortable, safe, shallow selves.

We do not offer the eucharist daily or wrestle continually with the things of God so that we can paddle safely along the edge of the seashore. If we want to experience the reality of God, we must be ready to strike out for the deep, to plunge into the heart of things. That is necessary for our health of mind, heart and body. People have a hunger of the heart that is never satisfied; they have a need which is never completely met to uncover the meaning in things. Human beings instinctively realise that there has to be something or someone who alone is capable of answering our deepest yearnings. We are made for the eternal, the infinite, yet it is part of our human tragedy, the result of human wilfulness, that we shy away from or shun what we know we want and need. And yet we cannot be whole, healthy or happy without a relationship with God. We thirst for some personal and intensifying experience of him. Deep inside each of us, often unacknowledged, is a space that only God can fill.

In the pattern of our lives, we need regular reminders of what is significant and opportunities to come to terms with our deepest needs. There is immense value in adapting to the rhythm of the Church's year. A time like Lent, for instance, is a time for reality and realism. I have tried in recent years to realise the desert experience that every Lent should be. We should be trying to come to grips with the questions that stubbornly refuse to go away: Who am I? Why am I here? Where am I heading? Has life any meaning?

In times of prayer and in carefully planned periods of withdrawal we try to make space and time for the truly significant and relevant. We try to vary the rhythm of life so that – like Moses in the desert experience of the Chosen People – we may have the opportunity to encounter the living God, the One who is. That involves meeting him in the desert and glimpsing the undying vitality of the fire which burns but never consumes. It is often a dread experience, it shatters our comfortable compromises. We sense that, and thus retain a certain 'horror' of God. We flinch from the mystery, the incomprehensibility and awesomeness of God. We prefer the familiar features of the idols we make for ourselves. They at least are containable. God on the other hand can be perceived as a threat. Surrender to him, which is absolute and reckless, with all its uncontrollable consequences, is seen as a kind of death.

If we reject the word 'horror' as too strong, we cannot deny that at least we are shy of God. We are made for him and need him desperately, yet, like Adam and Eve in the Garden, and people everywhere since, we try to hide from him, lest our nakedness and shame be seen. We seek escape in trivialities. We keep busy to drown out the whisper of God. We find substitutes sometimes even in good works or in the fervent observance of the outward forms of religious practice. What we cannot endure for long is the silence when God can speak. We dread that time when we become aware of what we really are and who God is: his vastness, wonder and mystery, our poverty and nakedness. We need to come alive. We have to become perceptive, focussed, coherent if we are to plunge into the heart of the mystery which is God. But, as we painfully know, we cannot endure too much reality.

3: Church Unity

Most of us make mistakes and fail to spot the obvious. Few however do it on a truly heroic scale. One of those who got it monumentally wrong was the late Irish Dominican, Cardinal Browne. Returning from a session of the Second Vatican Council and being interviewed at Dublin Airport, he was reported as saying: 'There'll be no changes; just a few alterations.' I fear he was expressing then what most of us secretly hope all the time: that the world we know, and have come to terms with, will never be fundamentally changed; that others, not us, will have to pull their socks up and change their ways; that we will be able to work the miracle of making omelettes without cracking eggs. Church-going Christians of every denomination are rarely radical; they value the status quo, the unvarying, the familiar. Yet the whole Bible, and certainly Christ himself, is wedded to the idea of change – that, after all, is what conversion implies – and to the vision of building a new world, a new creation, the kingdom of God that is to come. The change has to begin with me and within me.

To many of us older Catholics the ideal of Christian unity came late on the scene. Younger people may take it for granted but even they often fail to grasp the extent of the change it requires in attitudes and customs. We all ignore in practice the urgency of the need for Christian unity in a world of increasing unbelief.

Believers are given by God a special mission in life. We are called to be channels of his love and instruments of his grand design for the world and the whole universe. This is expressed vividly in the account Luke gives of Christ's witness in the synagogue at Nazareth, his home village. Our task like his is to bring the Good News to the poor, to proclaim liberty to captives, to give the blind new sight, to set the downtrodden free and to proclaim the Jubilee. We have to witness to the fact that God has forgiven humanity and has cancelled all debts. We are to be like the chosen people of old who were witnesses of God's treaty with his world, but we have to be committed to a new law, a more personal and radical morality. The world needs us to witness to God's unconditional love.

And what do we do? In practice we act as if the whole drama of salvation has been enacted in order to save our own souls. We are content that Christians remain divided and sometimes actively hostile to each other or at least suspicious of each other. We who are meant to be one body, a single living, breathing unity, a sign of forgiveness, reconciliation and love remain behind our defences in our separate castles. We will never convince a sceptical, unbelieving world since we lack credibility and fail to carry conviction. How can we unite and reconcile the world when we cannot unite the Church?

But things are changing. There are immense difficulties ahead but we have already in Britain passed four of the five milestones on the pilgrim road to unity. First we were in active competition with each other, aggressive, intolerant, deaf to dialogue. Then we moved to coexistence, prepared to accept each other's sincerity and right to live. We learned courtesy and mutual respect. After that we passed into co-operation with each other, working, especially at local level, at joint projects, sharing buildings and resources. We are now on the fourth stage of our road together. Following the historic conference at Swanwick in 1987 we as Catholics in England and Wales are committed – and that is a word charged with significance – to the achievement of unity. At this stage we have committed ourselves, in Cardinal Hume's words: 'to praying and working together for Church unity and to acting together, both nationally and locally, for evangelisation and mission'. That is the point of it all. We do not give ourselves to this task simply so that the Church may be one. It is that the world will be given peace, healing and a more secure future through us. We are then in the world as the visible, single Body of Christ.

Our commitment to Church unity which is the final stage of the process is important because it will be sign and sacrament of an even greater unity, that of our single, suffering world. No one may shirk from that task or refuse that responsibility.

4: The Church and Its Members

The worst kind of preacher is the person who relishes the prospect of setting the world to rights and putting people in their place. The self-important, the compulsive communicators, the infallible and the impeccable may occasionally impress but can rarely inspire and never spark the fire of the Holy Spirit. Excessive ego gets in the way. As an African proverb says: 'I can't hear what you say for the thunder of what you are.' Overwhelmed by the presence of God, Isaiah called out: 'What a wretched state I am in! I am lost, for I am a man of unclean lips and I live among a people of unclean lips, and my eyes have looked at the king, the Lord of Hosts.' Peter, stunned by the size of his catch after a night's fruitless fishing, is brought to his knees before Christ: 'Leave me Lord; I am a sinful man.'

Yet neither refuses the call; neither is paralysed or reduced to impotence by fear of failure. Recognising the force and intensity of the divine energy unleashed from within the deepest levels of their being, they react dramatically, decisively: 'Here I am, send me,' cries Isaiah. Peter, called to be a fisher of men, leaves everything and follows the Master.

These stories from yesterday are a challenge for each of us here and now. They tell us how each of us is called from the fumblings and frailties of our own egos to be witness to God's life and love and to be faithful labourers in the endless task of gradually transforming a bleak, greedy and loveless world into a kingdom fit for the children of God. That is the reality, the grandeur that lies behind the frustrations, difficulties and suffering of each passing day. There is infinitely more to us and to life than what appears on the surface. Our selves and our daily struggles are as significant and redemptive as the life and daily work of the unnoticed carpenter at Nazareth. That is because of his action within us, not because of anything we are in ourselves. The reality is that each of us – because we are baptised – become other Christs, share his life, are part of his mission and in union with him are caught up in his unique saving action.

The Church of today cannot be satisfied if 95 per cent of its members honestly believe themselves as laity to be second-class citizens of God's people. Many laity are content to be passive and part-time; at best they volunteer 'to help Father' in the work of the parish, but they shy away from wholehearted commitment. They fail to recognise their God-given responsibility and worth, and think that the Church is concerned only with 'churchy' things, the supernatural and the world to come. If told that their job is to build a better world, to renew the face of the earth, they would say: 'Who? Me? You must be joking. I'll be lucky if I scrape into heaven by the skin of my teeth.' That is not humility. That is a refusal to face the challenge and the calling of Christ. We are missing the whole point of our Christian commitment.

The truth is that the Church is more than an organisation, a hierarchy, a power-sharing democracy. It is a communion. Baptism pre-dates every other sacrament including holy orders, and is the most basic and important of all sacraments. Because we are baptised we are identified, made one, with Christ. We become, like him, priest, prophet and king. We share his mission from God to save the world. But each one of us has a sacred and specific duty: the ordained priest to the Mass, the sacraments and the word of God; the religious to a life of poverty, chastity and obedience in preparation for the final coming of Christ and the laity to offer up to God the whole of the secular world. It is the layperson's sacred obligation to become another Christ in the family, at work, in society, in politics. It is for the laity to make those worlds more human, more loving, more just. It is for them to discover God in the heart of everything.

We do not come to our task in a state of messianic exaltation. First, like Isaiah and Peter, we recognise the depths of our nothingness. Then, like them, we come to rejoice in the power of God's Spirit in our lives. We go out in his name, on his behalf, with his eyes, his power and love. We are always servants, always driven, but determined to play our part in our time and place, here and now.

5: Vocations

Vocations are not plucked out of thin air. They do not take root and grow in an alien environment. They spring from rich soil; they are the fruit of faith; they manifest the life that stirs in the Christian community; they reflect what the Spirit of God is seeking to achieve in the here and now.

That is why the present scarcity of vocations to the priesthood and the religious life is highly significant. It is at the same time disturbing, instructive and creative. The Second Vatican Council, in the 1960s, for all its reforming zeal, opened floodgates of discontent: the heady promise of a new freedom, the sweeping away of traditional restraints in the midst of a social revolution and wholesale change led to the emptying of convents and the loss of many pastoral priests. In the secular world the abyss has opened up to reveal the depths of disillusion, unbelief and moral confusion. But it does not add up simply to loss and despair. Through this whole process, the Spirit is leading us into a new situation and preparing us as a Church to confront a new challenge.

The future is not to be in the hands of the regular army of priests and nuns, leaving the laity as, in the past, to sit back or to respond only when summoned to play a minor part in the work and mission of the Church, a minor, delegated part for laymen, and even less for laywomen. There are to be in future no more battalions of clerical foot soldiers; no more troops of humble, passive religious staffing the schools, hospitals, orphanages and works of mercy. A new age is upon us that calls for total mobilisation, commitment at every level, the witness of Christian living in every nook and cranny of daily life. It is to be the age of the people of God in which all play their part as other Christs. The laity – willing or reluctant – has truly come of age and is being urged by God's Spirit to take proper responsibility as God's people for the work of God in today's world. The shortage of vocations to the priesthood and religious life is a kind of poverty that is, at the same time, an enforced purification. It makes priests and nuns think furiously about the real nature of their calling. At the same time it is an unmistakable indication from God that everyone has to be a wholehearted and full-time witness to God's presence in his world. There are to be no passengers and no idle hands on this stage of the Christian voyage.

Yet there remains an essential role for the ordained priest, essential work for the consecrated religious. For the priest there is the ministry of word and sacrament now more urgently needed than ever before; for the religious a witness of community, a lived experience of Christian poverty, chastity and obedience which most readily expresses the fullness of Christ in human living to which we are all called.

Will anyone come forward to be the next generation of totally committed ministers and wholehearted, selfless religious, to be the signposts to guide a pilgrim people on its way to the Promised Land?

In a changing world, in the midst of much uncertainty and self-doubt, the priest and religious are called by God and the Church to be prophets of the Absolute, men and women with far-seeing eyes to be the outsiders, the pioneers, the victims of sacrificial love. They have to be ready to let God live and love in them and through them. The next millennium of Christianity will be a new era with challenges, new vistas, and new forms of life and service, new ways of being Christ in a broken but redeemed world.

Priesthood and religious life are no calling for the timid, conventional, uncreative and the dispassionate. But such vocations cannot blossom unless the whole people of God share in the awakening. Our parishes have to become more truly communities of faith. We must learn to live boldly as the new creation. We have to remain open in prayerful faith to the prompting of God's Spirit within us. Then there will surely be a perpetual Pentecost, an endless outpouring of the power of God and of his life and love. Only then will we move closer to the realisation of God's presence in all things, the coming of his kingdom on earth.

6: More on Vocation

It is unnerving to live through an age of profound and rapid change. There are few guidelines and much confusion and uncertainty. No one is quite sure of the shape and meaning of the new age. Leadership then becomes a much more fraught exercise; commitment seems even more of a risk. It is scarcely surprising then that people are not in these days queuing up to volunteer for the priesthood and the religious life. In addition there is a prevailing atmosphere of materialism and unbelief; a widespread rejection of the values of self-restraint and celibacy and, throughout society in general, a fundamental reassessment of the role of women. It all adds up to a vocation crisis that will not be solved by appeals, posters or even prayer unless that prayer is part of a radical new approach to Christian living.

People today are no less generous and idealistic than previous generations. Perspectives and priorities however have changed. We have to stand back to distinguish the essential characteristics of the committed, celibate life in the service of others. We have to understand why in many respects it is profoundly unappealing to the new generation. We have to see how better to explain it and commend it. We have to think through ways of preparing for and perfecting the next generation of priests, sisters and brothers.

Recent years all dioceses and most religious orders have attempted to recruit vocations rather like other major employers. I myself have been involved in writing brochures and leaflets to explain the way of life, the qualities looked for, the spirit and history of some particular congregation.

There is in the vast majority of cases no substitute for personal contact, example and encouragement. We tend to be inspired by individuals not manifestos. Yet even individuals, charismatic as they may be, can often fail to convey the full depth and grandeur and the abiding richness of a life given entirely and unconditionally to God. In an age of uncertainty, more than ever, we are being called to be pilgrims of faith. We are to be free, uncluttered, ready to respond to new challenges and a new direction. It is not the task of future priests and religious to prop up the status quo.

I am coming to the conclusion that what we need more than anything else is an ever more profound sense of who God is. We have to glimpse something of the power and presence of the Spirit in all that exists. We need to realise that religion is not principally a matter of morality and observance of rules but a way of life, a spirituality that does not attempt to be angelic and otherworldly. The true believer rejoices to find God and self in all that exists, in the ceaseless manifestation of God's life and love in all things and at all times. We will perhaps turn the corner when we can convince ourselves and others that a life for God is not empty and most definitely not a flight from everyday life and relationships. It is instead a deeper, freer, richer living, a ceaseless exploration of the unity that lies behind all diversity, that unity which is God. To explore the Word of God, that which is written and that which is revealed in the lives of the people of God, to reach out for God through community worship and loving encounter with the risen Christ in the sacraments, all this becomes for the priest and religious a personal awakening. It is a new way of living life to the full, a loving that is unconditional and ungrasping. Then we can become through our personal witness and commitment a door through which others can pass to enter the sheepfold. We become a channel of God's life and love. We are the living bread for the life of the whole world, that with Christ and in him is daily blessed and broken and given.

To the searcher, both young and not so young, I would say: 'Come to the springs of living water all who thirst for the things of God and unending life. Drink deep and give others to drink.

'Come into the house of the living God and into the mystery of mysteries; plunge into the depths of God and spend your life creating beauty, deepening experience, unleashing the divine energies in others.'

It is a life and calling for the far-seeing, the loving, the passionate, the creative. It is the art of arts, the bringing to life and full flower what is divine in the human.

For those who have already made commitments, who have families and a vocation of their own I would say: 'The families who are part of this whole process should reflect on what they look for in their priests and sisters. They should cherish the distinctive ministry of religious and clergy. They should value it so highly that the ideal is made to seem for their young a way of life that is both hugely satisfying and eminently attainable.'

7: Belonging

If you hear anyone today comment: 'See how these Christians love one another', you can be pretty sure they are having a go at us. The words will be dripping with heavy sarcasm. The most frequent criticism levelled at us as an older generation, as church-going people, perhaps as professional Christians like sisters and priests, is that we are hypocrites, no better than our neighbours, not really committed in practice to what our lips profess. We recognise ruefully that we used to say the same sort of things ourselves about our 'elders and betters'. We can, of course, point out in mild self-defence that believing in God and his mercy is no guarantee of perfection. We are called as sinners to the table of the Lord. Conversion is a slow, painful and life-long transformation of our human selves. But, if we are honest, we are still left uneasy. There is something missing still. There persists a lack of direction, hesitation and doubt. We can see what Jesus Christ was saying, where he is pointing us, recognise the tremendous, life-determining choices before us. But then we wonder how realistic it all is. If we take him at his word and pursue the Gospel path, will the simple absolutes of the Gospel and our personal, passionate commitment to Christ leave us simple-minded in a complex world? Are we likely to become ineffectual, easy prey for any trickster or bully? Should we be at least nominal Christians, holding to some acceptable values, but guard ourselves against excess and sacrifice by keeping firm hold of our unsanctified and unbaptised common sense? Not here, Lord; not now, Lord; not as much as that, Lord.

These are real questions. It is why we sip so much diluted Christianity. It is why, to be honest, even those of us who have

staked our whole lives on the truth of Christ's teaching
still hold back part of ourselves. I remember at the 1985
Symposium of European Bishops the resistance there was,
especially among Eastern Europeans, to the idea that there
is among many people today a kind of 'partial belonging'
to the Church. And yet this is an observable fact. So many
go so far along the road; they accept some responsibilities
and consequences of being a Catholic but not others; they
cling to some doctrines and not others; they observe some
moral teachings but not others. Yet they insist they are
part of the family of faith. If we believe that the Church
is universal, of all ages and for all peoples, embracing even
the fallen and the wounded, who are we to unchurch them,
to deny their right to belong?

And yet the Christian Church cannot be shapeless, unprincipled, the lowest common denominator of belief. The
barque of Peter should not, cannot, let itself be blown off
course by the winds of fashion, by the gales of unbelief and
permissiveness, by sullenness and even mutiny among the
crew. We have to wrestle with this problem and we have
to recognise that the voice of Christ echoes still in our ears
and calls us to follow him, to stretch out to the limits of our
human selves, to reach unimagined heights. The one sitting on
the throne speaks: 'Now I am making the whole of creation
new' (Rev. 21:5). The Word of God is not, as it were, offering
us more of the same but this time in an improved form. It is
saying: 'There is a new world, a world of the spirit which
lies behind, shapes and transfigures the workaday, narrowly
materialistic world. You can be children of this world, but
you have to learn to live in a new way, to rely on different
life-support systems, observe new relationships, new ways of
behaving. You have to be ready to die to the old world,
the old ways, and come through into the sunlight of a new
world.' It is a high-risk choice. It is all or nothing. There will
be those around us who do not see what all the fuss is about,
who will ridicule or take advantage of us, and always within
ourselves there will be memories of the past, of our former
lives, of the fleshpots of Egypt and the securities of slavery.

Go back, be safe, anything for a quiet life. But then we look once again at the fascinating and compelling figure of Christ. We go back to the Gospels. We listen to the experience of our people and we have to wonder; can I let it change my life, can I let go my limited and selfish security? Is there a new life, a new dawn, a satisfying future?

Before we answer we have to look up to the altar and mark the figure of our Christ, the beloved, the hope of humanity, naked, tortured, put to death: not as punishment for sin, although he bore in himself the burden of our wickedness, but as a warning, a terrible warning, that there is a price to be paid for love. If you love as he did, as his Father does, it leaves far behind even exquisite considerateness, good manners, civilised behaviour. It is an absolute love, unconditional, unsparing, self-sacrificing, life-giving. It is terrifying love in its totality. It has to be so unquestioning. It is the love of Father for Son in the Holy Spirit with the whole human race identified and made one in the Son. It is this love which gives life to the new creation; it is the single principle and law of the new creation. It is, all at the same time, a challenge, a hope and a threat to our security.

When we come to the eucharist, when we claim to be Christian, we are laying claim to be sharer in that love, to be inspired and motivated by that love, to live life on the basis of that love. And yet would we die for the people in the next bench? Do we even bother to learn their names? Is our faith a private attitude or total conviction? Is it any wonder that people ask whether we really mean what we say?

8:   Achieving Peace

When we pause for the few moments of silence at the start of each Sunday's Mass and look back over the previous week many defeats come to mind, many difficulties, much frustration and discontent. Few of us seem to master the secret of inner peace or achieve calm purpose and unshakeable resolve. We continue to experience basic insecurity and self-mistrust. It is a state of mind and a spiritual malaise that afflicts us all at least from time to time. We would give much to find peace and that contentment which is worlds away from complacency and self-congratulation. We feel in our bones that this is what religion should give. After all, the prayers and blessings of the Church seem to promise peace; Christ claimed that he gave to his followers a peace the world cannot give. The Scriptures assure us that peace is flowing towards us like a river, that we are to be comforted like a restless child at its mother's breast, that peace and mercy are given to the new creation. Peace and the kingdom of God are apparently already within our grasp. The trouble is that 2,000 years after Christ we still live amid conflict, competition and inner alienation. The kingdom can seem an impossible dream. Is it nothing more than a somewhat pathetic illusion, that somehow, somewhere, 'over the rainbow', we will find all the answers, win all our battles and find endless reward for what we have endured? The world thinks of peace as absence of conflict. Christ on the other hand promises us a peace *in the midst* of conflict.

Peace will not just happen. We must seek it and achieve it although it remains always a gift – just as life itself is a gift. We do not create our peace, nor can we gain it by methods of positive thinking or transcendental meditation, although these can help. Peace is a consequence of something. This is clearly expressed in St Paul's letter to the Galatians (6:14). It follows only when we are ready to accept the cross and are willing to live through, with unshaken confidence and trust, the set-backs, the defeats, the little daily deaths and the final encounter with ultimate death. We are to surrender self-importance and self-centredness and live in the real world where we are part of a larger whole and of an ongoing life, where we share a 'divine spirit which shapes reality and brings it to richer existence through love'. We find life through letting go of our former self-reliance. We find peace by realising ever more vividly that our inmost selves share the life of God and his love and that others do as well. So we are never alone. We are not alien, at war or under threat from others. Together with the whole human family we are part of the presence of God in our world. Together we are meant to represent the power of the Spirit and to be channels of God's creative love. That is not easy to grasp. It is harder still to make it real in our lives and the inspiration of our actions. Unfortunately Catholics are no better than others in giving expression to the divine love that seeks outlet through them. One of the dispiriting experiences of life is to discover how contentious and unloving so many of our Catholic groupings can be. We are not conspicuous by our social compassion and racial tolerance. All too often we can be harsh and unforgiving. It points sadly to a lack of inner coherence and spiritual growth.

The story in the Gospel of the 72 disciples points to the way this peace of soul and entry into God's kingdom can be achieved. We have to take faith and a degree of commitment for granted as the starting-point. After that must come a willingness to be open to the call of Christ, to the demands of our inner spirit drawing us into action. We have to be ready to be moved; to go out from where we are; to share the truth and life that is within us. We have to be prepared to give and not wait to be rewarded; we have to bring blessing and hope to all we meet. If others reject us, well and good. It is not for us to punish or to feel resentment. Our sole mandate is to love. We must not be hindered by clinging to possessions, indeed we are to take no thought for the practicalities of purse, haversack and sandals. God will provide. We are on a risky mission but the only one whose effects will last since our names will be written in heaven.

Most Catholics will nod with passive approval at the vision but will feel that it is not for them. That might well be the vocation of priests and religious. They however have to earn their living and keep the wheels of the world turning. Nothing could be further from the truth. Without this broader vision and this call to mission, everything can end in tears and frustration. It need not, and should not be, the usual outcome. We are all called to glory and to share the life, love and peace of God. The kingdom of God is within each of us. It is not part of God's purpose that it should be fragmented and end in failure.

9: Peter

My mother, God rest her, could always be relied on to react with disgust when any television drama failed to end tidily, preferably with a happy ending, the loose ends tied up, all the questions answered. After all, a good story should always have a beginning, a middle and an end. But that is fiction. In life there are no endings, only change. Our experiences are muddled, without neat conclusions, leaving many question marks. Yet most of us are curiously uncurious; we tend just to let things happen; we do not ask questions; we do not sit down to work things out. If we live our own lives so haphazardly, what do we make of the past, of our roots? The book *1066 and All That* made sport of the half-remembered and hopelessly simplified events we recalled from boring history lessons at school. Yet history is not bunk; history is what made us: we should be anxious to gather up what fragments we can find and fit them together to make a picture of what really happened. It is so easy to distort and rewrite history, to explain the past in terms of the present instead of the other way round.

Which brings me to St Peter, who looms so large – especially in our Catholic thinking and living. His successor the Pope is for us the centre and guarantee of the unity of the whole Body. The Petrine ministry means so much that it is strange how little we *know* of the man himself. We have a lot of snapshots to go on, references here and there, vivid cameo portraits, and yet curious and yawning gaps. We know nothing of his childhood or early manhood, even how old he was. We know he was a fisherman, from the lakeside of Galilee. We know he had a house in Capernaum where Jesus lodged. We know he was married. We know he was among the first to be called by Jesus, that he emerged as spokesman, leader among the twelve apostles, marked out by Jesus as the Rock, as the one to feed the flock, to sustain his brothers. He was generous to a fault, impetuous, one who denied the Lord and yet was one of the first witnesses of the resurrection and a leader in the Jerusalem community. Then half-way through the Acts of the Apostles, silence. Tradition has it that he went to Rome and was executed by Nero and was buried on Vatican Hill. How he got there, how he carried out the Lord's commands, what became of his family, what he did – silence, frustration.

We know enough however to suggest he would have been acutely uncomfortable inside today's Basilica of St Peter – although he would have enjoyed the crowds, the sense of humanity coming home. He carried no tiara in the pack on his back. He would have been bewildered by the palaces on the hill. Today it would take him ages to understand the offices, the titles and the pecking order and the niceties of the Roman Church – hadn't his Master put all that to one side?

How then, 2,000 years later, should we remember him, make sense of his life, take our message from him? Three things, I suggest, stand out. The first is that he was always at the heart of a group, the centre of a circle. He was never a lonely leader and not the top of a pyramid. He is always seen, in the Gospels, as a member of a family, specifically a brother, son-in-law, partner in a fishing co-operative, and then as the spokesman, the big-hearted thruster to whom the others looked for encouragement. He was the witness, the Rock. He was always with people; the people of God, his human family, the Church. This is enough to remind us that we should never feel ourselves alone. We are always part of each other, always going to God with brothers and sisters, always able to look to others for support, encouragement and guidance.

The second thing Peter reminds us of is that we are called by God as we are. To be holy is not to be inhuman. To follow Christ does not entail being less of a human being.

Peter was human to a fault; a real person, rough, forceful, big-hearted, outspoken, sometimes too big for his boots, impulsive. He was sometimes scared but always enthusiastic. He lost none of that because he was called to serve his Master so spectacularly. So we must not idolise our pastor, even the supreme pastor. He too is the humble, enthusiastic, often fallible follower of the same Lord. Neither should we believe that to become totally committed to the Master requires us to become angelic. Our aim should be to become better, more intensely human, men and women.

Thirdly and finally, Peter was the Rock, because of his faith in the Son of God, because of his witness, the proclamation of the Gospel. He was called to that. His successors have that as their chief responsibility. We who are of the same stock, belong to the same people, have through our baptism and confirmation the same calling. In our Church there are no seats for passengers. We sit at Mass so as to get on to our feet, to walk out of the door and to carry the light of Christ with us wherever we go. We have to bear witness to the things which are unseen but utterly real. Peter reminds us of this. Maybe there will be nobody to write down our story but we have a part to play, however small, in the drama which is played out unceasingly on God's stage. A man's man, like Peter, would have found it very difficult to withstand ridicule and would not have been quick-witted and very effective in debate. He must have learned to control his temper the night he saw his Prince stand silently before the jeering soldiers. And under attack from the incredulous and the hostile he could offer only the truth of his own experience. In both these respects he can 'confirm his brethren'.

10: The Triumph of the Cross

I would not normally have switched on TV to watch the Wogan show in order to find inspiration or recreation. I happened however to be with friends one Friday when his guests were Lords Denning, Hailsham and Soper, who are all over eighty and all worth listening to for a variety of reasons. Lord Soper, perhaps the most significant Methodist of his generation, talked at one point about the whole purpose of being a Christian. The most important thing, he said, is to seek first the kingdom of heaven and its righteousness and everything else will be added. We are not Christians in order to save our individual souls but to be part of the struggle to save the world. I believe that needs to be hammered home endlessly. We will never begin to understand what the Christian faith is about and never have the chance to grow up spiritually unless we realise that it involves forgetting ourselves, our survival and self-interest and instead living wholeheartedly for God. We have to identify with him, sharing his love for others and all created things. If we can live and love without thought of return or of benefit for ourselves, we break through into a new dimension. It is like escaping the pull of gravity and being free to explore the galaxy. Of course, we have to grasp first a little of what God is and who we are. We need to escape from the lingering superstition that God is our personal lucky charm, our talisman. He is not someone who exists out there, up there just waiting to welcome me into paradise. God does not exist for me just to ensure my happiness and eternal salvation, but I exist for him, to be a continuing channel for his presence in the world, part of his plan to transform all creation into a living, loving unity. That involves self-sacrifice, a willingness to give one's all, the certainty of pain, rejection and the cross. 'Anyone who wants to preserve his life will lose it: anyone who loses his life for my sake that man will save it' (Luke 9:24).

This is not just a message for clergy, nuns, the so-called chosen souls. It is the secret of successful living for everyone, of personal healing and wholeness for all. It makes some sense of suffering, gives purpose to our disjointed and scrambled lives. It is very important to build up the whole picture, to see what we are supposed to be about. After all, we have but a single chance. Our few years of life then have to have meaning and purpose. When we come to the end, will it have amounted to anything? Why make the effort to live good lives, go to church, cherish a dream our neighbours do not share?

The answer is only to be found in Jesus Christ. To us as to the followers of his day he addresses the question: Who do you say I am? We should think carefully before we answer – because what our faith inspires us to reply not only determines what we believe about him but what we believe about our own selves. In St Paul's letter to the Galatians he is emphatic that we are sons of God through faith in Christ Jesus. There are no more distinctions 'between Jew and Greek, slave and free, male and female, but all of you are one in Christ Jesus' (Gal. 3:27–8). What he is, we are. What he came to do is, and remains, our sacred commitment and our task.

Christians keep saying, whether they really believe it or not, that everything that exists is good, is made by God out of love, manifests his infinite beauty, goodness and truth. Humankind, made in God's image and likeness, was meant to be God's partners in developing and unifying creation. Human knowledge and free will were perverted by pride and self-seeking and then helped to destabilise the balance and unity of creation. God, through his Son, showed what humans could be. He charged us with binding up the wounds of sin and selfishness. He wanted those who followed his Son to bring his love, his spirit, his intelligence, his energy to bear on the history of the world and on the other worlds in the cosmos. So far as we know, we alone share his life as spirit. We alone in the cosmos are self-aware, knowing, loving, capable of progress into the infinite. It is our task then to develop creation, to discover its secrets, to steward its resources, to harness its energies, to heal it and the wayward human race with love and in the light of God's revealed truth. The Spirit cannot be contained or subdued so life in the Spirit challenges, and threatens to undermine, all existing human power-structures, political, social or religious. Human selfishness and those who exercise authority will therefore resist and crucify the apostles of love and altruism, the bearers of the Spirit. But any death and defeat like Christ's will save the world in union with Christ's death and defeat. It will be our glory to make redemption real through suffering, through the cross and through the resurrection. It is for us, as other Christs, to realise and bring to fulfilment the inner harmony, goodness and beauty of creation, to live then for ever with the eternal Spirit in everlasting glory.

11: Reconciliation

Parents often have cause to lament that their children have drifted from Church and faith. They tend to blame themselves and wonder where they went wrong. When I was a younger priest it was possible to comfort the majority by saying that it was likely to be a passing phase and an assertion of independence. It was probable that they would come back at marriage and rediscover their faith as they settled down to raising a family. One priest, I read, used to say to parents: 'Perhaps they are only losing *your* faith and discovering their own.' Nowadays one cannot be quite so optimistic. The break is often decisive; the choices seem final.

In past centuries social pressures were often enough to ensure outward conformity. People went to church and accepted the public standards of Christian behaviour because others did. It was easier to follow the majority even if inner conviction and faith were seriously deficient. It was a religion of culture. Nowadays there is a multiplicity of options; we live in multiracial, multicultural societies. There is much less pressure to conform. In fact the social pressures favour unbelief and permissiveness. Those who believe and are committed do so out of personal conviction. For them there is now no longer a religion of culture but a religion of choice.

It is difficult to envisage a reversal of this trend. Society is no longer held together by shared religion and no longer feels obliged in its turn to uphold religion and its values. It pays at best no more than lip service to Christianity, and then marches to an altogether different drumbeat. While this can at times be distressing, it is healthier, more honest and more open. Religious belief is no longer identified with national identity, with civic respectability. We are losing the conviction of being a race chosen by God to triumph over our enemies. Where there are present-day exceptions as in the Middle East, the Balkans, Northern Ireland, the consequences are blood-curdling.

There is plenty of evidence in the Gospels that Jesus rejected traditional Jewish concepts of racial religion and of inherited moral and religious superiority. He welcomed tax collectors and sinners, told stories sympathetic to Samaritans, healed the children of pagans, warned that others would enter the kingdom before the chosen race and expressed astonishment at the faith of a Roman soldier. His attitude was so revolutionary that his followers, even after Pentecost, were unable to grasp that others beside Jews could be saved and be followers of the Messiah.

Jesus went out of his way to demonstrate that no one is excluded from the love of God and from the promise of life eternal. When he went out of his way to cure the servant of the centurion in Capernaum, it is important to remember that the Romans were the army of occupation. A modern parallel for Christ's words and actions would be a Palestinian praising and helping an Israeli officer, or a Lebanese Maronite taking a Syrian as a model, or a Bogside Catholic pointing with admiration to a British soldier. Two thousand years later we cannot claim to have made much progress in human understanding and tolerance. Perhaps today we no longer burn heretics and witches (although I imagine zealots still itch to do so). Today we may pay lip service to the idea of the universal family of mankind, but we still harbour tribal fears or resentment and practise discrimination against foreigners, ethnic minorities, other faiths, even, heaven help us, the other half of humanity whose only crime is not to be male.

We are emerging from centuries of religious isolationism, from attitudes which not only claimed that error had no rights but also regarded those in error as individuals and communities to be rejected, dismissed or at best devalued. Today we have not only to declare that the Church is the sacrament of reconciled humanity but also to act effectively in accordance with that declaration. In practice we do not behave as if each individual represents Christ for us. We do not act as if each individual, no matter what he or she may have done, never loses the shared image and likeness of God. We certainly do not behave as if each continues to be loved and cherished by God in every circumstance and so must be infinitely precious to us.

Catholics for example are not particularly active in work for racial and religious tolerance. Like others we discriminate, categorise, feel we can manipulate or dominate others. Or at least we do nothing about situations or injustice. We fly thereby in the face of the basic teachings of our Lord and Master. We like to imagine that piety and attention to personal purity and a self-defined moral code are pleasing to God while we fail to recognise him in others and in his creation. Thank God that he still shames us through the example of latter-day centurions, the Wilberforces, the Pankhursts, the civil rights activists, the feminists and social reformers of our day.

Many who are looked at suspiciously by modern scribes and pharisees will enter the kingdom before the self-righteous and religious.

12: The Body of Christ

The Bible is an earthy book about flesh and blood characters; it encourages us to think about God in very vivid and human terms. For the Jews, God was not abstract, Olympian, detached. He was to be found involved in every moment of their history. He was pictured often as a passionate lover, an ardent young husband, besotted with his bride, the people of Israel, rejoicing in her, never ceasing to call her back to her first love. Read if you doubt this the Canticle of Canticles; reflect too on the words of Isaiah: 'No longer are you to be named *forsaken* nor your land *abandoned*, but you shall be called *my delight* and your land *the wedded* for God takes delight in you and your land will have its wedding' (Isa. 62:4). It is a romance that reaches an incredible consummation when God himself becomes man and in Christ is to be for ever identified with the human race. The incarnation is not a fairytale but a love story. It opens up a new chapter in human history which is to continue till the end of time. The unfolding of God's love for humankind and for each one of us personally is so overwhelming and mysterious that most people fail to fathom its depths. Yet the realisation of it can change our lives.

When John in his Gospel tells of the marriage at Cana there is a simple narrative but many layers of meaning. The facts are familiar but John is hinting at mystery. Certainly he was hinting at the imagery of God and his bride. He wanted us to connect that with the life and ministry of Christ. God, the eternal lover, has come to his people and sealed their union. As Paul was to point out to his converts, Christ and the Church of believers are bridegroom and bride made one in love. Our broken humanity, the thin, flat routine of our daily living – the water stored in the six stone water jars – is to be transformed into rich wine, a whole new creation. When God became man in Christ it was but the beginning of a transfiguration of the human which is open to everyone prepared to believe and trust in the Good News. Those who are baptised are themselves changed. We are made a living unity with him, a single body. That is why the Church is called the body of Christ; why, as members of that body, we come to the eucharist to eat the flesh and drink the blood of the Lord and stand before God who sees in us nothing more or less than the living reality of his Son. And he loves each one of us utterly; gives himself to each one of us as gift, as life, as love just as he gave himself to Christ. We are not talking here just in picturesque, poetic images. This is the inmost heart of the Faith, the secret revealed only to believers and so rarely understood even by us. It has consequences which are concrete, personal and immediate. Remember how Paul, as he pondered this truth, taught in the first letter to the Corinthians (12:4–11) that when we are transformed into Christ we become a single living organism that exists in every age of history, every country. We die to selfishness and sin and become the new humanity, the living Christ.

We are made one humanity past, present, future. No death separates us, no distance divides. It is a single, living reality which spans the centuries. Living and dead together form the Body of Christ. In this body we share a divine equality – no class difference, no colour coding, no sex discrimination. Pope and peasant are equally loved by God in Christ: king and commoner walk side by side in absolute equality.

Then, as Paul teaches us so vividly, we each have our special role to play in the body: each of us embodying in our own limited way the infinite power and life of the Spirit. None of us is a sleeping partner; each is equally significant and important in God's plan and in his eyes. We are not in competition but in harmony. We need each other; we are needed by each other; we are truly interdependent. Through us and the baptised in every age and place, the

Word of God, Christ himself, is present. He works to bring all things into unity, working to heal, strengthen and guide. He is none other than God-coming-to-be in our evolving world.

13: Revelation

They say that God plus one makes a moral majority. Yet
I am sure that it is never easy to go against the tide.
Minorities – unless they huddle together for safety and
reassurance – tend eventually to conform. The ghetto or
cultural isolationism protects for a time, but social pressures
generally prove irresistible. It is no surprise, for example,
that the Catholic community, for generations a religious
and cultural minority, is no longer uniform and mono-
chrome in British society today. Even on crucial questions
of behaviour and moral principle, many Catholics take on
the protective colouring of their surroundings. Bluntly, they
tend to take their worship from Rome but their morality
from home. Catholics divorce as readily as others; they
seem to use contraceptives on the same scale as others; I
suspect that some are beginning to accept abortion or at
least to modify the traditional Catholic response of outright
rejection. To be a Catholic should mean not only to worship
in the time-honoured rituals of the liturgy but to embrace
wholeheartedly a vision of life and a set of values which
are not shaped according to private tastes and preferences
but are accepted as the teachings of Jesus Christ, handed
down and faithfully interpreted by the Church founded by
Jesus Christ himself. Increasingly, however, Catholics in our
society today seem not to be consciously Catholic in their
views and judgements. They tend to pick and choose from the
fashionable views around them. They ignore those teachings
of the Church which prove difficult and challenging in practice. They submit to the silent social pressures around them.
All this is entirely understandable in terms of sociology but is

spiritually dangerous. Eventually it could rot the very fabric of the Church for it destroys unity, coherence and effective witness.

The account in the Book of Nehemiah (Chapter 8), and the Pauline vision of the living body of all believers (1 Cor. 12:12–30) provide a necessary corrective. The Jewish people in the Old Testament are pictured as receiving with overwhelming emotion the revelation of God's law. That law was to be absorbed interiorly, was to become their very soul and shape their identity. It was from God. It was received with evident joy. St Paul reflecting on a new covenant shares his unique insights into what it means to be a true Christian. We are so united and identified with Christ as to form one body, with a single heart-beat, given life by the one Spirit of God who pours out manifold divine gifts on to the baptised without in any way endangering the unity of the body and its vital bond with the head. In this vision, we are urged to think of ourselves as united, coherent, forming ourselves after the model of Christ, open at all times to the Spirit of God.

We have in these two accounts the elements needed to build up a picture of the genuine believer, the true Christian. He or she is to be a person of integrity, honesty and goodness who is prepared to submit private judgement, convenience and self-interest to the will of God and to the law of God. He or she is willing to have that law interpreted and applied by the wisdom and experience of the whole people of God, the Church. He or she is a person who values the life and love received from God through the sacraments and especially baptism and the eucharist, who is open to the Spirit of God, loves the body of Christ and acknowledges kinship and solidarity with all who are baptised into Christ Jesus. True Christians are willing to accept by faith the richness of a vision unattainable by human reason; they rejoice in the fellowship and the diversity of the people of God.

Only when we are steeped in the revelation of God in Christ, when we have had poured into our hearts the inexhaustible love of Christ, when we are strengthened by the power of the eternal God present in Christ and, through him, in the Church, then, and only then, are we able with Christ, and in his name, to face the miseries and distress of our times and to proclaim the Good News with clarity and conviction. We, like Christ, are sent to preach good news to the poor, to heal the world's wounds and to set the downtrodden free. We can do these things, for which we too have been created, only through him, with him, in him, in the unity of the Holy Spirit and in the fellowship of the Church.

This is a far cry from the self-hearted, wavering and confused believers we often know ourselves to be. Yet I know of no other way of life, no other value-system, no other attempt to give meaning to things that even remotely compares with the revelation of God in Jesus Christ. Here we can find an unceasing source of life and love that can transform our lives and our society. To be faithful to Christ, to obey his Gospel, is the only way to escape the tyranny of fashion and to be free from the slavery of being little more than children of our own time.

14: Present Witness

It is commonplace to remark that we are living in a time of bewildering and rapid change. Things unthought of, undreamed of, a few short years ago are now part of daily life. We tolerate the casual destruction of many hundreds of thousands unborn; we discuss calmly the possibility of creating embryos for research and experimentation; we take for granted the collapse of family life, as one-third of all marriages end in divorce, leaving a million and a half children in one-parent families. Terror stalks the streets; torture is the preferred tactic of the oppressor. All around us the beliefs and values of our Christian inheritance are questioned and ridiculed – and not only by agnostics and the unprincipled. We could be witnessing the death agony of a particular civilisation and a particular age or, more likely, the birth pangs of a new generation and a new culture. Death and resurrection are the rhythmic pulse of God's dealings with his world and his people. Ultimate victory is assured but never painlessly and always through death.

Who then will be the prophets and apostles of this new age? Who will turn the searchlight of truth on to the pretensions and the falsehoods of those who peddle new solutions to ancient problems?

It is helpful to look back into history to see what happened at other times of deep crisis. When the Roman Empire collapsed under the weight of its own corruption and the onslaughts of the barbarian tribes, it was the followers of Benedict who created new communities to salvage the treasures of the past and to discover how to live a genuine Christian life of prayer and work. When the Christian civilisation of the Middle Ages in its turn collapsed in the sixteenth century as new knowledge challenged old beliefs and superstitions, and as the unity of Western Christianity was shattered by the Protestant Reformation, new religious orders, a reformed parish clergy, a better instructed laity emerged to inherit the past and express it anew. The counter-Reformation was a form of resurrection.

In our own day we need a gigantic new effort to serve our own generation and our own time. There are some who fear that we are being overwhelmed, that we have not the priests and religious to fight the battle against evil and darkness. Will they be the prophets and leaders? The contemporary crisis is not about clerical vocations. The future of the Christian people will be secured by a new way of being the Church. Already the seeds have been sown.

Since the Second Vatican Council in the 1960s we are being reminded all the time that the Church is not just something we belong to: the Church is each one of us. Each Christ, ordained or not, is reminded that at baptism we were each of us consecrated to God and made – in the words of the sacrament itself – priests, prophets and kings. We each were called to be the people of God. We were marked out then, and by virtue of our baptism, to be wholehearted followers of Christ, upholders of whatever is good, just, righteous. When we were confirmed, we consciously accepted the responsibility of standing up for the truth and the Gospel.

The way forward for us today is clear. If each of us is faithful to our baptism and confirmation, if each of us receives Jesus Christ into ourselves at communion and lives in his light every day, the forces of darkness will not prevail and a new era could even now be at hand. But it means mobilising all our resources and seeking allies. There is no room for passengers. One and a half million committed believers should have stunning impact on the life of this country. They should challenge the very bases on which our society is built. But who today fears one and a half million church-going Catholics? Do we make any significant difference to the life and quality of life in this country? The Church does not have a simplistic, politicised programme, but we are, at least in theory, committed to building the kingdom of God in the city of man. But would anyone notice?

If the Church is to be revitalised, if the laity, the people of God, are to be prophets and witnesses to Christ in the land, we each need deep experience of conversion. We need to learn better how to pray, how to appreciate the Mass and the sacraments. The Gospel has to become our own; it is a whole way of life. The parish has to become alive as we learn how to relate better to each other, to rely on each other's support, to become the real community it so rarely is. We need to trust the real but partial communion which already exists between baptised Christians and find ways of expressing it in action. That is the challenge before us.

The Second Vatican Council was the starting-point, not the conclusion, of a process of renewal which has been necessary to meet the challenge of the times. Change has occurred often in the teeth of mute opposition. Some would say that grass-roots Catholicism has not yet owned the new spirit, the new vision of what Christian living demands of today's Church. Patient, courageous witness and teaching will be the priorities for a generation to come.

THE INNER TRUTH

Introduction

It takes the best part of a lifetime to arrive at willing ownership of one's inner self. For most Christians this is usually a lonely adventure. There is a marked lack of spiritual guides, especially in the typical parish. Few these days are prepared to search out the books that might provide sustenance and guidance. There are limited opportunities to develop a life of prayer. All too often those of us who carry responsibility for the spiritual well-being of others find ourselves embarrassingly inadequate for the task.

Fifty years ago when I first ventured into the junior seminary at Ushaw I was exposed to the full rigour of a way of life that today would excite amazed rejection. We all encountered a deliberate attempt to wean us from home and our natural background. Everything was subjected to change, even our raw northern accents. We were trained to be emotionally independent and yet responsible to authority. The avowed intention was to make us into well-drilled troops of the Church Militant. We had to become men relied on for our unquestioning loyalty, obedient to our superiors, ready to endure hardship and frustration, to go where we were sent, to expect nothing and to work until we eventually died in harness. It was by no means an ignoble aim; it certainly suited the temper of the time.

The glaring defect was that it paid little or no attention to the emotional, psychological and, ultimately, the spiritual development of the individual. Living an isolated life in the countryside, without newspapers, radio or cinema, cut off, apart from two holidays a year, from family and former friends, warned away from 'special friendships', we were trained relentlessly for celibate solitude. As a contemporary put it much later: 'When we had finished we knew how to resist lust but had no idea how to cope with love.'

With hindsight it was a system doomed to failure because it was in such marked contrast to the crusade on which we had ostensibly embarked which had love at its heart and which aimed at building a living, human community, the Mystical Body of Christ, which was meant to witness to the world 'how these Christians love one another'.

The celibate has to learn slowly and often painfully how to combine love and concern with detachment and lack of possessiveness. But everyone else in his or her own life-situation needs help to mature emotionally, psychologically and spiritually. Too often people remain emotionally scarred, inadequate, handicapped. We all need to create and keep clear an inner solitude and space where we can be most truly ourselves because we are in thankful harmony with the Beloved.

There are spiritual guides who like to stress how utterly isolated we are; we come into the world alone and depart alone. In point of fact both examples of alleged solitude are singularly inappropriate. The love of two people brings us to birth, and devoted medical and nursing care and the support of family and friends surround and enrich most births. As death approaches we are usually also the focus of great attention, tenderness and solicitude. We come into life as part of a family; we depart leaving behind those who genuinely grieve for our passing. Our individuality, our inner world, is not something that distances us from others but makes us kin. Our humanity cannot flourish except in communion.

The greatest of all life's adventures is the quest to become real. This is not achieved by the pursuit or the winning of pleasure, power and possessions. It is essentially the discovery of the divine depths within ourselves. We the re-deemed have been given life for one reason only, to be loved and to love. God created us, to change round the words of the old *Penny Catechism*, so that he might know us, love us, serve us and be happy with us for ever in heaven.

The sole purpose and ground of creation is God himself who is pure, unending *agape*, perfect love. He creates in order to give himself away; nature exists so that it can be cherished by God; in all its forms, vegetable, mineral, animal, it reveals God. In that creation, however, humankind enjoys a special place. Throughout Christian tradition there has been the constant insistence that 'the glory of God is the human being fully alive'. Pope John Paul II has defined Christianity itself as 'deep amazement at mankind's worth and dignity'.

It is an essential element in our redeemed spirituality to reconcile, harmonise, seek unity and growth. The joy of our making and of our healing and transformation is to be found not in eternal fulfilment but in the everyday circumstances of the here and now.

1:   Divine Depths

They say that seeing is believing; yet most of our progress is due to the fact that we gradually realise that nothing is as simple and as obvious as it seems. Common sense for centuries was satisfied that the world was flat, that the sun and the moon circled the earth, that the stars hung in the dome of the sky, that material things were solid and substantial. Everything was just what it seemed, neither more nor less. We now know that we literally cannot believe our eyes or trust our senses. The reality is more mysterious and exciting. We are anchored by gravity to a planet that hurtles constantly round the sun while spinning on its axis. Relying on our senses we confidently called ours *the* sun not realising then that our solar system is part of a galaxy made up of more than a billion other suns. Hard solid reality is largely made up of emptiness and the interplay of energies. Little wonder that we care not to think too often of things as they truly are. We prefer instead to bustle through our earthly existence, taking for granted even the wonders that human genius is beginning to fashion out of the stuff of creation. We rarely pause to think that we move in a world that is alive with the magic of silent sound and music, where invisible pictures are beamed through the air into homes everywhere. If we have a transistor or television set we can tune into the ceaseless sound and vision that is part of our environment and yet is inaudible and invisible to the ear and the eye. For the first time in history we are freed from the constraints of time, space and even death itself. We can see events taking place on the other side of the globe; we can hear music and song and witness drama in recorded form, bringing into our lives from anywhere in the world the greatest entertainers whether alive or now dead. We can cross the Atlantic by Concorde in four hours; we can fly to the moon; we can orbit the earth in a matter of hours. The human spirit and our creative genius are discovering the secrets of creation, unlocking energies and potential undreamed of in the past. We are achieving unbelievable results; but one last frontier remains. There is one line we cannot cross unaided. By our own efforts we cannot unleash at will the divine power within us, cannot grasp the inner reality which, despite appearances, is our real self. Only twice in human history has the curtain been fully lifted and the truth revealed. Once for 40 days the disciples of Christ were made aware of his risen life, physical yet transformed; once on Mount Tabor the inner glory trans-figured the familiar features of the man who was Christ.

It would be a brave and foolish man or woman who would stand up today and say: we have reached the limits of our knowledge, have exhausted all the possibilities. If we stand in awe before the marvels of our natural world we are only now beginning to appreciate the inner glory that is deep within all things, the limitless horizons in search of which throughout history we are making pilgrimage. At the heart of all reality, behind the familiar, the tangible, the observable, is an energy, an intelligence, an endlessly loving purpose. We are convinced that Jesus Christ embodied in his own self and by right all that energy, intelligence, love and purpose; in a sense, he earthed the divine in the human. He did not represent a radically different human existence. He was one of us; he ate, laughed, loved, talked, wept as one of us. But also alive within him was the divinity he now shares with all of us. He was, and is, literally God's sacrament: an effective sign of the reality he represents.

After God took flesh and blood in him, it was a small step for God to enter our world as often as need be by means of bread and wine, water, oil, the touch of a human hand, all signs and symbols verified by the Word made flesh. Most times the reality can be grasped only by faith, and despite appearances. Only occasionally, as on Tabor, faith is swallowed up in vision; the flame and the energy burst forth. But the reality is every bit as real when no one sees the glory, when we can be misled into believing that everything is just as it seems.

It is important to try to find time, space and deeper faith to realise that there is an inner fire, a bright glory, a life and a love within us which are trying to find greater expression. Tabor may be remote from our experience, but I am convinced it is not meant to be the privilege of a few. God came in Christ's humanity, so that humans might realise their origins in God and their destiny. The secret of creation is that all things pour out of God and are then to return to God. We are in the midst of marvels; we tread on holy ground; we should ask the Lord to let us from time to time see and still live.

2: Being in Love

It is irritating to be told so often that love is blind. In fact, the opposite is true. Only the lover has eyes to see the beloved as God himself does, from the vantage point of unconditional love. Love and life are cause and effect. Only love brings to life what to others is unseen and lifeless. Love discerns beauty where others see only the familiar. It enables the lover to delight in the loveliness which lies at the heart of everything that exists. Only love truly appreciates that God is in everything and everything is in God. All is transfigured because it is seen as a reflection of the endless beauty that is God.

Life too is changed out of all recognition when the realisation dawns that the one known and loved in turn knows and loves us. And the ultimate bliss is to appreciate that there is Another who knows and loves with overwhelming intensity, without limit and without need for any 'why or wherefore'. It is a basic insight of Christian faith that we owe our very existence to God's love for us. We are because we are loved and loved eternally and unchangingly. God can do no other since he is love.

I can still remember the moment of revelation when I truly came to realise that God loves even the damned. In the midst of what constitutes hell he still loves endlessly those whose minds and hearts have freely closed themselves to him. To say that God is angry with anyone or punishes anyone is a misleading way of describing what happens when people try to walk out on God. If God could conceivably be absent it would mean utter annihilation. When I tried to share my moment of discovery with a friend he replied, 'But that's what I thought the

Creed meant when it declared He descended into Hell.'
One man's astonishment is another's platitude. But the
point for me is that now I know.

The word 'love' is used so glibly and superficially to
describe a human emotion that it is easy to forget that real
love is more a state of mind, a way of relating to people
and things. It is a fact of life which habitually determines
my responses. It is not so much a feeling as an energy and a
state of being. It persists unchanged despite moods and
passing fits and fancies. Love is a grateful and wondering
response to the awareness of being loved. It depends on
that understanding of reality which we gain from Jesus
Christ.

The Christian insight tells us that reality is not alien or
hostile. All created things, all human beings result from the
creative outpouring of divine love. They reflect in some
measure the endless truth, beauty and goodness of God.
They are patterned on the Godhead. They are the bodying
forth of all that he is because they are made in the image of
God the Son, the Word. They are therefore loved endlessly
and unconditionally by the Father and that love is the Spirit.
All is in God and so the universe is a work of love since
it is conceived in love, embodies love and expresses love.
Creation is essentially friendly and is our necessary and
nurturing environment. As human beings, in a particular
way we reflect in our essence at all times the life and love
of God. That is why we too should love even our enemies
without 'a why or a wherefore'.

We are so used to the fickle, the wayward and the conditional in human loving that it is well-nigh impossible for
us to grasp the absolute nature and awesomeness of God's
love for us. In him there can be no shades or grades of
loving. He cannot love and partly love. He loves each of us
as he loves the saintliest and the most gifted of creatures.
And then in Christ he has the astonishing audacity to say
to each of us: love others as I have loved you. No one is
to be excluded even if they are enemies. We are to refuse
judgement and condemnation of others because we must see

God in them as well as in ourselves. There is no need to
scour the earth in search of signs, miracles or manifestations.
The greatest of all signs and miracles is the gift of God's
love.

3: Forgiveness

The word Pharisee is now taken as a term of personal abuse. That is an oversimplification of the evidence we find in the Gospels. It would be quite wrong to think that Pharisee simply equals hypocrite. It is not always a case of public responsibility masking inner corruption and secret wrongdoing. It was much more complicated in the religious scene in which Jesus moved and which he knew so well.

Most people remember the story Jesus told of the Pharisee and the Publican in the temple, their contrasting attitudes to God and to prayer. The judgemental and complacent are compared unfavourably with the humble and self-accusing. Both are types still instantly recognisable and both in their own way are genuine. Christ does not deny that the Pharisee is in fact generous, just, faithful to his wife and scrupulous in the observance of fasting and paying dues to the temple and its priests. He is a model citizen, an upright and honourable man. He is a committed believer and the sort of person who would be welcomed on a parish council, a board of directors or as a parliamentary candidate. He seems to be the salt of the earth but with one glaring fault. He is conscious of his virtues and looks down on moral weaklings who are not as he is.

The Publican is neither good nor worthy. He betrays his country, collaborates with the occupying forces, extorts money from his own people, is callously indifferent to justice and other people's sufferings. His one saving grace, as Christ tells the story, is that he knows he is a moral disaster and a social leper. He casts himself on God's mercy. Christ judges him to be better off than the local worthy, the model citizen, the pillar of the parish.

If we really let the point of that particular story sink in, it might seem at first that Christ's teaching is quite outrageous and morally irresponsible. Perhaps it might appear so because few of us fully appreciate the novelty and liberating truth of the Gospel of Jesus.

He wants us to understand that we do not in the first instance have to win God's approval, earn his love, avert his anger. It is not as if God is a detached observer of the human drama, sitting in the stalls watching us perform briefly on the world's stage, applauding some of the players and rejecting others. In fact he loves and identifies with all his sons and daughters. From the beginning he does not see in us either the Pharisee or the Publican. Instead he recognises in each one of us his own image and likeness. He sees in us the features of Jesus Christ his well-beloved Son and he loves us as he loves his own self. He can do no other.

This is not to say that virtue and a good life are not important but that we can claim no credit for what we are or do. Everything is a gift and proof of God's unceasing love. Literally, there is nothing which has not been given to us freely and generously. Our life itself, our personality, talents and appearance are all derived from our parents and genetic inheritance. The air we breathe, the food and drink that nourish and sustain us, the very planet we inhabit, all that makes our lives possible and enjoyable are not of our making. We may say we earn our living but that is a very loose expression. It ignores the essential contribution of others and the underpinning of God who is all in all. We have nothing to boast about since ultimately all depends on God's creative love.

It is important to understand that nothing we can do appeases or impresses God. Publican and Pharisee alike have to acknowledge their utter dependence on him. Both must throw themselves on his mercy and love.

Without question that comes hard for human beings who so delight in their independence. In the last analysis, though, it is a profoundly enlivening and liberating truth. Nothing, not even our sins, can ever separate us from God or deprive us of his abiding love. We have to assure ourselves that we are living in his world, his creation. He surrounds us every minute of our existence with his infinite tenderness. We have to relate to others as he does, not judging, not repelling, but always making every allowance and providing the opportunity for a fresh start. We need to see through the outward appearances to the inmost reality which remains unchangingly beautiful and of God.

4: Growing through Relationships

Marriage breakdown has reached epidemic proportions in contemporary Britain. Explanations of various kinds are brought forward in an attempt to determine why lasting commitment and stable relationships are increasingly rare in society today. Certainly one of the reasons why many marriages fail is to be found in the breakdown of communication between the couple. The art of relating at anything more than a superficial level has never been properly learned.

It is usually easy to identify the married couple in a restaurant or public house. They are the silent ones unless they are entertaining others. Married couples sit silently side by side in their motor cars unless quelling a backseat rebellion by their children. It is a sign of emotional burn-out and not of that profound contentment and silent sharing that arises from a union of mind and heart. There is nothing left to say because they believe they know everything there is to know about the other. They no longer listen either to words or to body language.

The need to communicate effectively with others is at the root not only of a successful marriage but of any meaningful relationship. It is just as important for our spiritual as for our emotional and social lives. We need to find time, space and sharing with God and with our own inner selves. Cut off, we remain deaf, blind and locked inside the shell of ourselves. We fail to grow and reach maturity.

I think this is the real meaning of the familiar scene from the Gospel where Jesus is being entertained by Martha and Mary who each have their own idea of what is important. Martha usually comes off worse when the two sisters are being compared. Perhaps she should be chided gently not for what she did but for the way she did it. After all, to prepare a meal, to serve it attractively, to see to the needs of an honoured guest is an expression of love and concern. Without bustling Martha, Jesus would probably have gone hungry. Mary showed her welcome and appreciation another way. Her rapt attention to Jesus meant that the joy of his presence could be savoured long after his departure and be a source of continuing growth. Of the two sisters Mary is commended for choosing a life-giving relationship with their guest. Martha was allowing activity to block her total attention.

The incident emphasises the importance of sharing and communion in the spirit. In a relationship what matters and what endures is the enjoyment of the other's presence and the sharing of mind and heart.

In a traditional Japanese home the family welcome a guest by placing a single flower in his or her room, not a vase or a bouquet. They explain this by saying that the guest and not the flower brings beauty to the room and adorns it. They do not want to smother that beauty with competing flowers. That displays a delicate sensitivity we too often lack.

When Mary sat at the feet of Jesus to drink in his every word she paid him the supreme compliment. Her absorption in him was not passive but totally involved. She gave him every ounce she had of devotion and attention. She grew by her listening. She drew strength from his wisdom and words. There is here a lesson for our own relationships and growth.

We relate to God and the world of the spirit by prayer. There is no admission to that world by the mere recitation of words no matter how sublime. Prayer is presence, rapt attention, the opening of one's whole self to the other, real communication. All too often prayer is regarded as a one-sided recitation of needs, thoughts and feelings. In practice we deny that there is anyone listening because we leave no time or opportunity for a response. We tend to believe that God listens only when he grants us our wish. Our whole approach in fact signifies that we believe God to be at our beck and call, to be subjected to our arm-twisting and only believed in and accepted if he does our will, not his own.

Communication with God has to grow in stillness and silence. Later we can go about our business without interrupting the state of union between us. We learn to live in the light of the Beloved. But that is the result of an intensive process of sharing and mutual awareness. We have to imitate Mary before we can afford to be as busy as Martha.

Real prayer which is a true process of communication will on occasion be profoundly disturbing and produce unforeseen results. That can happen only if we dare to be still and allow God to take hold of us his way. Perhaps we keep chattering and call that prayer because it is safer to drown out his voice and not let him become for us the way, the truth and the light. Perhaps too we are afraid not only of confronting the Lord but even of discovering our true self behind the masks we offer the world and ourselves.

5:   Growth in Love

There is cynical insight in the saying: 'Nothing is impossible if you don't have to do it yourself.' We can casually subscribe to many ideals, provided we are not called upon to flesh them out in our daily life and by our own efforts.

Nothing could be more familiar and yet less observed than the Gospel teaching to love the Lord God with all our heart, soul, mind and strength and our neighbour as ourself. It seems amazingly simple in theory to urge whole-hearted love of God and a lively and constant concern for one's neighbour. The difficulty of fulfilling this double commandment becomes painfully obvious the moment it is really taken seriously. The basic law of love is sometimes portrayed as an easy, candy-floss-sweet option. Love and let live; love and peace: the universal cure-all. Yet it is deceitful to pretend that any kind of genuine love can exist without sacrifice and pain, without the cross. Any married couple, any parent, any faithful priest or dedicated sister can tell you that the precious gift of self, which is the heart of all union, friendship and love, has to be given freely but always at a price to oneself. It involves a kind of dying, a letting go of self and a willingness to sacrifice one's own interests for the sake of the shared good of both partners.

Yet our deeper instincts, our better selves, insist that this Gospel wisdom is the key to life. I recently came across some beautiful words of Teilhard de Chardin. He said: 'Someday, after we have mastered the winds, the waves, the tides and gravity, we shall harness for God the energies of love. Then for the second time in the history of the world, man will have discovered fire.' He was stretching out his mind to embrace the totality of God's kingdom, that 'civilisation of love' which Pope Paul VI used to speak of with such passion and such wistfulness. Fire is a sign of the Spirit and we are made Christians by the blood of the cross and the fires of Pentecost. We stay faithful despite all the odds, we struggle to be better Christians because that same Spirit has claimed us totally for himself and we try to be committed to a life of love and loving service. We are already to some extent 'kingdom people'. We are gradually and often painfully being transformed from within by an energy which is literally inexhaustible, ever self-renewing. We share in that overwhelming life which brings every-thing into existence, which is the everything in everything that we call God. We have the power and the life of all things within ourselves and yet we remain stiff and inert.

We sense instinctively that we are 'living and partly living'. We barely begin to tap the potential that is in each of us. We accept with resignation our broken lives and sinful selfishness in ourselves and others. We lack the conviction and the vision to commit ourselves to the fires of love and by doing so set others on fire. We need look no further than the many failures we experience in our fumbling attempts to bring children to adult maturity. As an American doctor recently wrote: 'Too many children get everything they want and nothing they need.' Because we fail to find our inner selves, we never really discover God. Consequently we never manage to love others without a huge shadow of self-love blotting out the beauty.

Is it all then hopeless? Are we condemned to endless frustration, to loveless sterility? God forbid. Every day offers the possibility of new awakening. Every period of silent and centred prayer can deepen our awareness of who we really are. Every Mass, each eucharist, can transform us impercep-tibly into a living offering of love. Like the blind beggar, Bartimaeus, we can plead for sight, for the 'wisdom-eye', the eye of the heart. We can grow in love only if we let go our tunnel vision, see all reality as Christ saw it – as a single and ceaseless outpouring of the beauty and love which is God. Then we can let that life flood into every pore of our being; we can cast away fear and learn really to love.

6: Resurrection

Teilhard de Chardin once wrote: 'The great objection brought against Christianity in our time and the real source of the distrust which makes whole blocks of humanity impervious to the influence of the Church has nothing to do with historical or theological difficulties; it is the suspicion that our religion makes its followers inhuman.' I think he has hit a nail firmly on the head. The other source of objection and distrust is the suspicion that our religion also diminishes our zest for life, takes the joy out of living and reduces us to drab, guilt-ridden zombies. That is an image we have ourselves helped to build up. Catholics sometimes say: 'It's a hard religion to live by but a comforting one to die in.' That remark is piercingly revealing. It demonstrates the depths of our alienation. For most Catholics sanctity means doing without more and more, ridding oneself of material and physical comforts, detaching oneself from worldly preoccupations and retreating into silence and incessant prayer. Life, the world around us and the business of daily life are considered largely irrelevant or a temptation for the believer. Religion is a matter of withdrawal and rejection. All that fails to take account of what Easter and the resurrection, the central belief of our Christian faith, really mean. It is an attitude that refuses to recognise the whole point of religion. We remain blind to the fullness of life and the reality of the unending love which both surrounds us and should become the energy at the heart of our own lives. Christianity is not in fact about rejection and denial but about being born again as a real child of God. It is about life. It is about being more fully human. I wish I had always known that.

What makes all the difference is genuine faith. Living faith can transform believers into a community that pools its resources, that cares for each of its members, that shares their work, life and future. Faith can take hold of a cautious, sceptical individual like Thomas and bring him to his knees in wonder and adoration. For many of us, however, our Catholic faith is quite often a fairly passive, uncomprehending assent to a set of truths. Doctrines are presented to us by the Church and are perhaps received with respect but not as the star to steer by, and certainly not as an enthralling vision of all reality, of all life and death. For many of us faith is not wholehearted trust and commitment. We are simply not prepared to stake our lives and our souls on the truth of Christ's words. We do not live by an understanding that is authentically and unmistakably derived from the unique view of the world that is Christ's and Christ's alone. At the pivot of Christian faith is the Easter happening, the rising of Christ from death. The Church witnesses to that truth. I now frequently have to ask myself whether that faith determines my life. Can I, and do I, find life and myself in the light of that faith?

St Paul wrote: 'None of us lives for himself alone, none of us dies for himself only; if we live, it is for the Lord that we live, and if we die, it is for the Lord that we die. Whether we live or die, then, we belong to the Lord' (Rom. 14:7–9). That can start me on the road to understanding. The death and resurrection of Jesus Christ are not a truth, or a saving event that is confined to religion or relegated to the abstract and unreal. It has to do with all life and reality; it gives us a key to unlock every door. It is of unique importance for us both in our living and in our dying. What it says to us is this: Be at peace. No matter what anxiety, fear or failure threaten your life, take courage. Jesus Christ is no mere man, not just a sublime prophet and teacher. He is the true image of God, the true image of humanity, the very embodiment of God in our world. I have to struggle to see what this means. He is that Word of God in whom all things are made. Everything is of God, is made out of love, is a single whole, is destined for glory, is fundamentally friendly, is of everlasting significance and value, is part of the wholeness of God the Son. Created things, ourselves included, never lose their place in God's love. The human spirit chose to disregard this love and unity, claimed its independence, wrenched reality out of joint, chose death and darkness in trying to be like God. But despite human sin, God can never let go. When the Word of God took flesh it was to prove to us that life and our real humanity can only be found in love and unity. We are not to rejoice in isolation and self-assertion. We are to find healing and wholeness in union with Christ – which means with the whole of humanity living and dead, with the rest of restored creation. When we realise that *Christ means life*, the fullness of humanity, there is no longer room for competitiveness, jealousy or fear. We share. We take delight in God's gifts to others as well as to ourselves. We see God in others. It becomes our delight to release in them and affirm generously all that is of God. We lose our dread of death for we are one with the fundamental principle of all life, with Christ who is not subject to death, who lives for ever. We rejoice that we are irrevocably part of God's eternal outpouring of life and love. That, and not our petty pride, should be the root of our sense of our own significance and confidence. Christ's life and death have opened our eyes to what the stupendous truth is: that God is in all things and all things are in God. Or to put it in Pauline terms, 'Christ is all, and is in all' (Col. 3:11). We do not belong to death but to life. We should not be in retreat from our human selves but free to be fully human and to live. That is the Easter message which has meaning for the whole of life. It recalls to us that here and now – and always – we share eternal life.

7: The House of God

Never mind all the fine words of politicians trying to convince us that we have turned a corner and everything is coming up roses. If we want a single image or instance of the state of our nation we can find it in far too many towns and villages of this country. It is the locked-up church. Locked-up apart from Mass and service times, not because no one wants to worship or pray but because of vandalism, theft and the danger of desecration. There has been in my lifetime a dramatic and sickening loss in the sense of the sacred, in respect and in any real awareness of right and wrong. Society stood by unconcerned as faith in God and in Jesus Christ was challenged and undermined; we could get along fine without the dogmas of the past. But now people throw up their hands in horror as standards crumble, violence erupts and human dignity is defiled and degraded. Now the politicians blame the Churches for not preaching morality and values, but how many come to church to listen and are they not already converted?

The churches stand locked. But there are some of us who care. There is faith. The Church survives and will always survive and we can take heart from other symbols, other images. Recently I celebrated the anniversary of the consecration of the chapel where I normally celebrate Mass. It was resplendent with candles and flowers, alive to the sound of music calling the faithful to keep alive a love and faith and union with God that will sustain and enrich their lives. There are enough churches, enough believers to change the world.

There are many who cannot see beyond the end of their noses, who are blind to the beauty that stares them in the face every moment of their lives. There are those who are deaf to the messages of hope, of love, of life that God speaks to them in every word he utters, in created things, in lives of goodness and service, in his revealed truth in Christ. There are many crippled by greed, selfishness, fear. But there is beauty, there is truth, there is health and freedom and lasting joy and we can encounter it daily if we know what to look for. God sent his Son as the divine physician not to the healthy but to the sick. We have only to open our doors and ourselves for him to enter and to heal. He wants us to open our eyes, to listen with care and learn to live and to love at every level of our being.

He is saying to us that there are around us wonders beyond all our imagining, a reality hidden from the blind and the deaf but beckoning us on. We have to learn that God wants us to live at a new level of intensity and perception. He wants us to be free in his kingdom but first we must learn how to breathe and function in this new dimension. We must learn the secrets of our new creation. We must learn how to pray, to see with new eyes, to understand what lies behind what seems obvious but is deceptive. Prayer is really a matter of perception, an attitude of mind, a state of attention.

The whole world is sacred but a church is a privileged point of encounter with God, a place of rendezvous with the eternal. Just as in our daily lives we need moments of conscious concentration, of centering, of stillness, so in our world we need holy places, places of prayer, of beauty, of intensity. If we disregard the sacred and bypass the holy, we miss everything that can make life a lasting delight. We should treasure our local church but see it always as a door that opens into a whole world of meaning and fulfilment. Here we encounter God but here too we meet each other at a deep level of appreciation and fellowship.

Here time does not stand still; here life is not shut out; to here we bring our lives and our world and they are given back to God who enriches us so constantly and so incredibly. And from here we go out into our world.

8: The Bread of Life

When I was a young priest I used to take Holy Communion to an old gentleman over 90 years old whose father had been ten years old at the time of the Great Famine which almost destroyed rural Ireland in the hungry 1840s. His father used to describe the dead lying where they fell in the ditches by the roadside. There used to be a belief in Ireland that the grass never grew again where a famine victim lay dead – they called it the hungry grass. The failure of the potato crop caused the famine, the last and the greatest recorded in these islands. We in Britain have never known hunger on that scale. It takes an effort of imagination for us to imagine starvation, to put ourselves for example in the skins of those broken and starved bodies revealed when Nazi concentration camps were liberated at the end of the Second World War. In more recent times we were appalled at the hideous pictures from Ethiopia in 1985. Here again, drought and crop failure led to massive loss of life, unspeakable suffering.

Our relative plenty, our lack of immediate obvious dependence on the land and its harvests have led us to comparative complacency; we never worry where our next meal is coming from; we do not live literally from hand to mouth; our physical diseases are more those of affluence than of hunger. But even for us plenty may prove precarious; there is no certainty that our increasing prosperity will continue endlessly. We understand more about nature than all our ancestors, but we have displayed such recklessness and insensitivity towards our finely balanced environment that we may one day pay the price.

Still we probably find it hard to place ourselves in the

shoes of those in the Gospel whom Christ fed by the lakeside in their thousands. Here were people who knew real hunger, who lived on the knife-edge of starvation and felt at the mercy of the elements. It was for them an experience of unexpected delight and new hope when they were fed and filled at a time they expected to go hungry. They saw the harshness of nature held at bay; they sensed the presence of God's power and recognised his love and providence. Little wonder that in the Gospel story they wanted to make Christ their king.

The whole point of the story is that Christ did not want to be their king but their very life. He tried to use their hunger and their feeding to lead them into a new awareness, a new consciousness. Food is not everything, physical fulfilment is not everything; there is much more to human life, much more to our being fully human; there is a deeper, truer, richer reality underlying appearances. Our very existence as thinking, loving human beings raises much greater expectations and the promise of a greater destiny than full stomachs and money in the bank. Christ satisfies hunger, for the moment, to show that there is a deeper, more constant hunger that only he can fill and for ever. It is a hunger for the eternal, for a life and a love that have no limits and no end.

On rereading John's account I am left with a single image; the image of a loving, trusting God who in Christ cares endlessly and unconditionally for everything and everyone he has called into existence. He is a God who can be trusted to meet our physical, material needs in so far as that is good for us. He is a God who has no favourites but gives life and love to the thousands who go in search of him without distinction, making them one family, a single people. He is a God who says: come alive to the truth that you are, like Christ, my sons and daughters; when I see you, I see the face of my only Son who became like you and brought you into a single whole, one body. I want you all, with him, to share my glory and my eternity, a life you have never dreamed of.

But that invitation, that call, falls now as then on deaf ears. Because it needs faith and a leap into loving arms.

9: Healing

Today people are rarely confronted with the physical evidence of death. It takes place in hospitals or hospices and only rarely at home. People disguise the reality and avoid speaking of it directly. It is the unthinkable, the ultimate tragedy. God's wisdom contradicts this flatly: 'Death was not God's doing, he takes no pleasure in the extinction of the living. To be, for this he created all' (Wis. 1:13–14). The whole of the Bible is rich in images of life; it is after all the book of life. One of the images I dearly love is to be found frequently in the Psalms. The very first Psalm says of the just man: 'He is like a tree that is planted by water streams, yielding its fruit in season, its leaves never fading.' People who knew the desert rejoiced in abundance: 'They feast on the bounty of your house, you give them drink from your river of pleasure; yes, with you is the foundation of life, by your light we see the light' (Ps. 36:8,9). With our roots in the living water, we are likely to survive and to bear fruit. In psychological language this may well mean: dig deep, water flows underground. In religious language it recalls to our minds the basic truth that God is within – within us, within all living things, within all that is. We are to find him there through inner awareness and stillness and not through frantic dissipation. The medieval mystic Meister Eckhart described God as the great underground river which no one can dam and no one can stop. The Christian faith urges us to be like God our Father, endlessly alive, ceaselessly creative, giving thanks for what we are given and giving back life and love in the same measure that we receive it. It is such an astounding and beautiful thing just to be, to exist, to be aware, to be able to transmit the energy of love and life by all that we are and do.

There are further echoes of this teaching in Mark's Gospel where he tells of the raising from the dead of Jairus' daughter and the healing of the woman with the issue of blood who touched the hem of his garment. For me the lesser miracle is the most revealing. Both affirm that God became man to heal, to give life, to lift up from the defeat of disease and death. The raising of Jairus' daughter, though spectacularly effective, was the result of direct action by Christ, but what are we to make of a healing that came when, filled with faith, a woman touches the hem of his cloak? Is she saved by the release of healing power within herself by faith? Or are we to see Christ as so alive, so charged with vital energy that he created around himself as it were an energy field that could restore health to anyone able to tune into it? Who knows? We are still only presently and partially exploring the possibilities of life, of being, of energy. All we can be sure of is that those in total communion with God have access to a vitality and power that is literally deathless. This is the meaning of the miracles sometimes worked by the great saints. The ministry of healing, so long ignored in the Church, is the beginning of a recognition that God is the life of everything and that this is manifest in the little things as well as the large. But to be part of that process one has to be prepared to die to oneself, to renounce self-determination, to seek nothing outside of God and nothing in addition to God. But that, of course, is not a denial of life but a surrender to the ultimate reality, to the All in all.

10: Mission

When people lose hope and a reason for living they die. Sometimes they have died a long time before the day of their funeral. What keeps us alive and makes us grow is hope, a sense of purpose, a reason for living. Some people never live to their full potential. Others are prepared to live and work for the sake of their families. Only a few are prepared to make sacrifices for the sake of a cause. Few realise that they are called to renew the face of the earth, to live and die not for a dream but a vision, a vision of what the world could be, should be, of a world fit for the children of God. The reason so few of us live lives of energy and effectiveness is that it never dawns on us how indispensable and magnificent we are in God's eyes and what part we are called to play in God's plan for his world. We can live and die without realising the real point of our existence, without ever waking up to the fact that in our own special world and in our own special way we can change our own lives, help change the lives of others, bring new life, light and hope into a lot of dark places.

One of the great jokes in world literature is the story of the half-crazed Don Quixote and his servant Sancho Panza setting out to live a dream in a real world which constantly defeats him. But in the Gospel we read how the Lord Jesus sends out his disciples on a mission that might seem to some as crazy as Don Quixote's but which in fact helped to change world history. Jesus had recently been rejected on his own homeground. Undeterred by failure he sent out not twelve Don Quixotes but twelve Davids to slay the Goliaths of disease and darkness. They were to set out with the minimum of support and provision. They were to take their chance as it came, living off the land, moving on when they failed to get a response, travelling light. Had they first weighed up the odds they might never have set out on their mission. But they went because they were sent and because they had absolute trust in their Master. That surely was why they won through.

We, like them, have been singled out by God for our own personal mission in life. We, like them, seem to face impossible odds, the near certainty of incomprehension, ridicule, hostility, rejection. But the mission is not ours but God's, and all too often we fail to recognise that truth or its consequences. We fail to let God be God. We forget that he is the reality within all realities, that he is seeking constantly to be born more fully into our world, to stand revealed in the minds and hearts of men and women everywhere. It is not for us to bring God into our world, he is there already. But the forces of human pride and self-sufficiency which obscure and inhibit his presence need to be challenged again and again and revealed for what they are, a recipe for living death. We challenge them principally by our consistency in living the Gospel of absolute love and being willing to see God in all things and all things in God.

In this we follow more closely the way of Jesus. Yet all too often today we lack any sense of urgency and purpose in following Jesus Christ. All too easily we lose sight of him amid the distracting detail of daily life. Unlike the apostles, we fail to hear his insistent demand that we spread the Good News, drive out our contemporary devils, heal our sick society. We carry too much baggage from the past and are too painfully conscious of our past failures and sins. We prefer the familiar and all too often mistake it for faith itself. We expect defeat even before we come to grips with the enemy. We dissipate our energies in petty squabbles, jealousies, internal dissension. We fail to be transparent. We simply do not expect to be able to change the world.

The end result is that very often we are content to regard faith as a private treasure, to be savoured in secret, not as a thing to be shared. The proposed Decade of Evangelisation to climax this millennium has not captured many minds or inspired much enthusiasm among British Catholics. It is likely to be stillborn. The mental and religious habits of a lifetime cannot be reversed at a word of command. We will have to try to convince ourselves over a considerable period that the faith we have is always personal but never private. It is meant to be shared in order to conquer death and overcome evil in the places where we live. Like the apostles, Christ today calls me positively to action, to be his hands, and eyes and ears and heart in challenging entrenched injustice and wrestling with the powers of darkness, the unclean spirits. We are called to heal and restore and that means we have to be involved. We must not simply bewail the sin but befriend the sinner. There was a catch-phrase current a few years ago that if we are not part of the solution we are part of the problem. That has meaning in this context. God will refuse to accept our endless excuses for inaction. We are not necessarily called to devise a new Utopia but humbly and bravely to try to apply in every circumstance the basic law of Christ: to love in all things as God our Father loves, without a why or a wherefore, without thought of benefit or reward, but simply because God is God and all things are to be loved in him.

11: **Pain**

One Friday in September 1986, a priest friend of mine was killed in a car accident on a motorway in the North. It was a personal tragedy, a loss to those who knew him, but so routine as not to be regarded as a news item. The bulletins, the newspapers, record in grisly detail the daily tragedies, the massive catastrophes that destroy lives, poison the environment, leave thousands stricken and bereaved. It is a savage irony that a society which has pushed back all the frontiers of knowledge, which has revolutionised medical care and surgical techniques, should be uniquely guilty in our time of crimes of violence and calculated cruelty, of genocide and oppression. And, for all our knowledge, we still stand helpless in the face of illnesses like cancer and AIDS and when confronted by so many natural disasters. The non-believer jibes: 'How can you believe in a loving and omnipotent God?' And we in our distress ask *why?* And we hear the echo of those who stood by the cross on Calvary and scoffed: 'If you are the Son of God, come down from that cross and we will believe.'

I recall Calvary on purpose. In his dereliction and distress Christ must have wrestled with temptation. But he could not wipe away the pain, he could not cancel the passion and step down unharmed. That might have appealed to Hollywood phantasies, to Superman fiction, to those responsible for *The Last Temptation of Christ*. It would have stunned the onlookers, but it would have betrayed his mission and perverted faith. The presence of God in the world, the nearness of Jesus, is in no sense a guarantee of miracle-working, in no way takes away the harsh reality of suffering. It does not produce a sunlit, never-never land where there is no death, no grieving, no loss. The cross of Jesus Christ tells us that faith does not take away suffering but it helps by giving it some sort of meaning and hope. Christ's passion proclaims that we can find life in the midst of death, and that love is the ultimate secret. It is the only creative response to life.

The first misconception we must rid ourselves of is the image of a remote and ineffectual God, somehow detached from the agony of life. Calvary and the cross tell us of a different God, a God who became vulnerable, limited, subject to pain, rejection, distress and death not only in Christ but in all suffering humanity. He cared so much that he identified with us, did not flinch from suffering, submitted to dereliction and execution, an outcast, reviled and despised. He is a God who came among his people and will never leave them until the end of human history. If suffering is a mystery, it is one shared by our God. That should make us pause for further reflection. There is no depth of pain and rejection where our God has not been before us.

And why? I would not want to be dogmatically certain but I believe we have to think along a double track. The first is this: the cross and Calvary show us the Good News that God not only exists but that he loves. He loves before we do anything to deserve it; he loves no matter what we do, however we respond; he loves without question and without end. He loves and thereby makes us special, worth dying for. It is proof, perhaps the only proof, that God is love and that the secret of all existence, all experience, all history, is love. We have to take a dramatic leap of faith to say that underlying all the horrors and despair of the world is the inner secret of love. Only the cross justifies us in making that assertion.

The second track is this: Calvary and the cross, the free sacrifice of Christ, plunge us deeply into one of the great mysteries of our experience, bring us face to face with a truth that is verified at every level of life. It is not just a religious truth, but a fact of life that only by dying or by being prepared to risk death do we live. All living things die, but only in this way is new life possible. Only if we are ready to die are we free to live and to enjoy life in its richness and fullness. All loving is a kind of dying, a denying of oneself in order that something new, a creation of life, might be possible. Only if we go boldly into the very jaws of death, and walk trustfully into the dark, can we discover life and emerge into the light. Calvary is swallowed up in the brilliance of Easter. Despair followed by hope, defeat by victory.

But most of us fail to understand and refuse to believe. We dread the pain, flee the inevitable, remain locked in our selfishness and isolation. Only if we are liberated from our fears and realise that God, present in our lives, is a guarantee of victory and unending life, can we emerge enriched and strengthened by our experience of suffering.

I would not dare to claim that these two lines of thought will solve all the problems and render us fearless and serene. What I do say, and from experience, is that by patiently following these we will come to realise we are not alone, that we are loved in and through the pain, and that somehow all this is part of the pattern of love and living, infinitely mysterious though it be.

12: Forgiveness

As a priest with a long and varied pastoral experience I have
often shared with people their distress and isolation when
they are unable to forgive. We are rightly appalled by the
class hatreds and the bitter antagonisms that persist between
nations. But that should not surprise us. People, individually
and collectively, find it hard to forgive, to break the vicious
circle of retaliation and revenge. Lives are ruined by it; much
slaughter and bloodshed are caused by it. The instinct to
make someone pay, to settle scores, is deep in all of us.
But Christ insists that there is a better way. It is possible
to heal, to forgive, to start afresh.

Part of the problem lies in our attitude to ourselves. Let
me explain. Quite often you hear it said that the golden
rule of the Christian religion is to love other people as we
love ourselves. Well, yes and no. That can be positive and
helpful advice. It is, however, usually irrelevant because it
avoids a very real and basic problem. Loving others as we
love ourselves is fine if our relationship with ourselves is
healthy and sane, if we are at peace with ourselves, truly
and properly love ourselves. But how rarely that happens.

All of us are of course self-regarding; to an extent, self-
obsessed. Not all of us realise it. It is usually only recognised
if it takes the form of blatant self-love, crass self-promotion.
But even those who seem, and are, shy and withdrawn,
depressed or over-timid, are still often preoccupied with
themselves and still have themselves in the forefront of
their attention. The trouble so often with us is that although
we cannot take our eyes off ourselves we do not like what we
see. We have learned over the years, either through childhood

experiences or from what life seems to have taught us, that we are inadequate, unlovable, insecure. We regard ourselves with barely disguised dismay and disdain. Inside we are prey to fear, liable to dislike ourselves, to find there nothing of value. If we are unable to accept ourselves as we are, if we are not able to love ourselves then we will never be able to fashion healthy, joyous relationships with others. We will find ourselves hating in others what we know to be inside ourselves. We will project into others the fears, loathing, anger and distaste that we really feel towards ourselves. It somehow makes our inner life and self more bearable.

The consequence is that if we are not able to forgive ourselves we will find it hard, if not impossible, to forgive others. And as we experience conflict and unhappiness inside ourselves we will certainly find it writ large in the people we meet, the situations we create. We will be almost compelled to see others as a threat, as people to be dominated or manipulated. We will find it natural to compete against others, to judge them usually quite harshly, to fend them off and to subject them to ourselves.

In fact what the Christian golden rule means is something quite different. Elsewhere in the Gospels Christ is recorded as saying: Love one another as I have loved you. Now immediately we are in another world and will begin to make sense of so much of Christ's teaching. We do not, could never, earn God's love. He loves us first, loves us always, and without conditions or possibility of change. From eternity he sees each of us as images, reflections of himself, like his Son, Christ, because we are each called to that divine destiny. We are forgiven absolutely, without reserve; the reconciliation has been made by Christ's unswerving love and obedience until death. We are loved, forgiven, exalted; and we look out in the joy and trust of that love on a world redeemed, on other people equally loved by God, equally reflections of his glory. So we, loving them as we are loved, can hold nothing against them, do not have to wait until they earn our confidence and love, will forgive them endlessly and love them even when they hate us.

An impossible ideal? Not if we let the reality of our forgiveness really sink in and share generously the freedom and joy of the children of God.

13: Ageing

I remember once in Chester years ago preaching about the Mass. Later a lady called on me to ask for books on the Mass; she felt she had much to learn. Not a remarkable story except that the lady in question was at the time over 90 years old. Intellectual curiosity, a thirst for knowledge, is a way to retain youth and vitality. I read recently a book by another remarkable lady, a psychiatrist still active at 95. In it she recalled advice given her 50 years before: 'This year and every subsequent year attempt to achieve three things. Make a new friend, acquire a new skill, learn a new language.' Even if only one is acted upon it delays the onset of ageing. You may notice that they refer to heart, head and hand. Friendship awakens love, language bestirs the mind and a new skill unleashes creative energy. All are ways of coming alive, of engaging the whole person in the joy of being alive.

All this is not simply geriatric counselling; it is a spiritual and religious imperative. It has everything to do with the truth that God is a living God, that God is the energy which awakes into being everything which exists and that God wants us to live ever more richly and totally. This may sound an obvious set of assertions but they convey a message which few of us ever fully grasp. Most people do not associate religion with having a great time, with living life to the full. For them religion is a turn-off, a denial, a restriction: grim-faced and accusing.

Yet again this is another example of standing truth on its head. Because if we want to see people living and partly living in the city of the living dead, we have only to look with clear eyes at the passing scene. It is strangely sad and somewhat sinister to see people deliberately shortening their life expectancy and putting their health at risk with alcohol, cigarettes, drugs of one sort or another, or by dicing with death on the motorways, or poisoning themselves with those processed foods, so aptly named 'junk food'. And all this in the name of freedom and fun. If we want to see the death wish at work we have only to look around us.

14: To Work for Peace

One Sunday in 1986 I was standing by the Wall of Death in Auschwitz concentration camp in central Poland. There Polish prisoners in the early days of the Second World War faced German firing squads. On the left were the shuttered windows of the cells where prisoners waited execution. On the right the block where some were starved to death or asphyxiated. Later we were to go to the second Auschwitz camp some four kilometres away where four million people – 90 per cent of them Jewish – were gassed and then cremated in those hideous years of Nazi tyranny, 25,000 each day. Two weeks later I was in Assisi with a national pilgrimage of young people to be part of the Pope's day of prayer for world peace.

It is hard to imagine two places more starkly contrasted than Auschwitz and Assisi; the one dedicated to death and the brutality of power; the other to life, the joy of creation, the service of others. The two places help to focus on the reality of our present situation. Usually we stand too close up and find it hard to grasp what is really happening.

The concentration camp, the huge concrete gas chambers, the crematoria, the acres of wooden huts where victims were huddled in terror until their turn came; these remain a grim warning of the world we can build when we turn our backs on God. The middle years of this century – the 30s and 40s in particular – were a time of horror, not only under Hitler but in the Stalinist terror which was responsible for the genocide in the Ukraine, the Gulag Archipelago. They marked the utter bankruptcy of a society without God, without humanity, without compassion. They left us the legacy of the bomb – the threat of annihilation which paradoxically proved to be the only thing to check the outbreak of further war. But it was an uneasy and fearful peace. The end of the Cold War was not the result of conversion but of economic collapse and the endurance of the human spirit. But we were brought to the brink; we have peered into the abyss. We have seen what man can do to man. We must not be mesmerised by danger, endemic violence and difficulty. There is a better way; there is still hope. But we ourselves have to be part of the solution.

Assisi – and what it stands for – holds out a promise of a better future. It is a place of breathtaking loveliness. Its steep cobbled streets and its flower-decked houses make you feel that you could turn a corner and chance upon Francis himself, the lover of poverty, the poet and priest of all God's creation, the passionate believer in the infinite worth of each individual. It was an inspired move of the Pope to call to Francis' hometown all those who believe in God to pray for the future of humanity. On October 27, Pope John Paul, like medieval popes before him, called for a day of universal truce. He asked that the guns fall silent, the bombs be laid aside and the whole world stand still, just for one day, to listen, stretch out, draw back. There is a better way. It is a way of peace, of solidarity, based on the unshakeable conviction that we are one human family, brothers and sisters, children of God. We have to work out what we do when we disarm. When we reduce our armaments, lay aside our weapons, what next? Then we have to change our hearts; then we have to look at others with different eyes.

If we want peace, we have to work for it and we must not wait for others. In a funny way, the demands of peace are the same for ourselves as for governments.

First of all we have to learn never to degrade or demonise our opponents by making them into devils. They remain our family.

Then we have to work out how to reconcile our national self-interest with the needs of international justice. It is a problem that runs through life. It is present in the smaller details of our personal lives. How to believe in partnership when I am tempted to dominate in order to survive. How to make compromises? How to live and let live? We do not know all the answers. We must continue to ask the questions and to set ourselves the task of discovering ways to ensure that all can sit at life's table, able to preserve their dignity and assure their future. If we do not, we die.

And finally we have to understand more profoundly what St John meant when he said, 'The Truth will set you free.' We must be able to embrace truth, to follow its consequences, to accept that Truth-reality is God. It is never to be feared, always to be respected. No friendship, no relationship can be built on a lie or survive in a climate of untruth. Our world, our society often accepts the lie and lives it. The devil is the father of lies. Over the gate of Auschwitz still stands the Nazi lie. Cynically, brazenly, it says to this day *Arbeit macht frei – Work sets you free*. And this over the entrance not to a labour camp but to a death camp. Evil masks its true face. So we must never be slaves to deceit.

Peace then is our business. Peace is an enterprise to engage all those of goodwill but especially those who believe in God. We pray and live for peace.

15: Peace is a Personal Choice

When in 1986 I made a pilgrimage to Assisi with 140 young
people from Great Britain and Ireland, we took part with
thousands from round the world in a unique and intensely
moving day of fasting, penance and prayer for world peace.
You could be forgiven for missing it in your newspapers
and on TV here. It was almost entirely ignored. I am told
that the Jeffrey Archer scandal attracted 15 minutes in the
news bulletin that night compared with less than two minutes
given to Assisi. But make no mistake: when Jeffrey Archer
is long forgotten, Assisi will be remembered. Its importance
was quite extraordinary. Why do I say that?

There is no single issue of greater importance for the future
of the world and its peoples than that of peace. Peace is more
than absence of war and more than disarmament. Peace
is positive and is built on justice, right, order, trust and
forgiveness. To talk of peace is not political and does not
stray from the things of God. We must not be schizophrenic,
nor unreal. If we believe in God, we have to accept all
the consequences of that belief. We must live our lives in the
light of that belief and work for a world like the one God
intended. That necessarily involves commitment to the work
of justice and the service of peace.

On October 27 the world flocked to Assisi. Representatives
of the entire Christian family, for the first time in history,
and leaders of the other religions of the world again, certainly, for the first time in history, came together at the
invitation of the Pope. They came to the birthplace of St
Francis to fast together, to pray each in their own way
and to commit themselves afresh to the cause of peace.

Even the Red Indians came, the Crows from Montana, to smoke the Pipe of Peace. Assisi was a sign that men and women everywhere acknowledged their shared humanity. They are one family. Everywhere in the human heart is a longing for a future that is free from fear, from oppression, from the threat of annihilation.

But Assisi was more than a single, dramatic event. It has to be the start of a process. Believers round the world must refuse to accept the inevitability of conflict and bloodshed and unite in the cause of peace. We are then in a whole new political situation, manifesting irresistible pressure that world leaders simply cannot ignore for too long.

Mutual mistrust, antagonism and desire for revenge have been used to justify nuclear deterrence, insane levels of defence expenditure and limited use of force to achieve political ends. We are often told by our political leaders: if you want peace, prepare for war. Instead we should say: 'If you want peace, work for a just world.'

I say this because it became clear at Assisi that simply disarming is not enough. It would certainly be an immensely encouraging sign of a readiness to break the deadlock. But when we have laid down our arms, how then do we build the peace?

Good Pope John XXIII had his answer ready. Twenty-three years ago, in his encyclical *Pacem in Terris* – Peace on Earth – he taught us that peace can only be built on four pillars: truth, justice, love and freedom. Without them any peace is only a truce, maybe a peace of exhaustion or of tyranny, but true peace has to conform to righteousness, respect, liberty for our own lives as well as for world affairs. They have to replace greed, selfishness, aggression and revenge. Mere self-interest can never motivate true peace. We can stress to our leaders that all these things matter to us. They must not be allowed to get away with the disastrous attitudes that have never worked in the past. There is a better way.

A final thought makes us realise our own part in the work for peace. In Assisi, Pope John Paul reminded us that we have not done enough when we simply pray for peace.

'Peace,' he told us, 'is a universal responsibility; it comes about through a thousand little acts in daily life. By this daily way of living with others, people choose for or against peace.' Prayers should indicate the choices we have made. Do our lives show we have opted for peace? Our prayers are real only when our words are consistent with our lives.

16: Love and Live

Anyone who knows me even slightly will confirm that I am not one of nature's compulsive shoppers. Sometimes it takes quite a while for a trend in the shops to hit me between the eyes. Recently, though, even I have noticed that the commercial world is taking up Mother's Day with a growing but suspicious enthusiasm. I cannot help noticing that, for instance, commerce at Christmas deafeningly beats the drum for family while at the same time every other social pressure seems intent on undermining and devaluing family life. So when the shops and commerce generally try to make money out of motherhood I wonder why they are paying such attention. Society today seems hell-bent on asserting women's inalienable and precious right not to be a mother. Abortion is an assertion that unborn life is disposable, that motherhood is fine for the willing but a disaster for those who have other plans. Today we have an economy built on the two-income family. Motherhood is treated as a hiccup in the progress of a career. The raising of a family is placed low on the scale of desirable occupations. So perhaps the most charitable conclusion is that big business is paying tribute in its own confused way to the stubborn human instinct that wants to honour life, is grateful for the gift of life, and loves mothers and fathers who have shared with us this most precious blessing. The human family cannot for very long deny its own self, the reason for its being. It must eventually give proper pride of place to human love, the miracle of birth and the joy of living. Already the selfishness of the recent past is beginning to cause a lopsided society, rapidly greying, and unsure how to prop up its future prosperity as the potential labour force is seriously depleted.

In recent times the Church has been ridiculed and reviled for its defence of human life and its passion for the family, the integrity of married love and the sanctity of procreation. In the 1960s the prophetic Paul VI stood out almost alone in his defence of the principle that there is an intrinsic and unbreakable connection in the act of married love between that which unites a couple personally in mutual fulfilment and that which at the same time may spark off a new human life. Pope Paul was saying that we divide union and procreation at our peril. If we separate the two, making loving an end in itself, or emphasise procreation at the expense of true tenderness, *in both cases* we create a monster that devours. The Church is trying to hold a precarious balance despite all misrepresentations from within or without. Love has to mean commitment; commitment to life as well as to each other. Human loving expresses and makes real the creative love of God for all that he has made. To be a mother or to be a father is a deeply moving affirmation that life and love are bound up together and that God intends us to love and live and give life to others.

All this might appear strange coming from an ageing celibate priest who has chosen not to marry. Priests and religious have renounced the blessing of family and children but only out of an even more passionate commitment to life and love. We do not undervalue but want to intensify and purify the *quality* of that same life and love. By trying to strip ourselves gradually throughout life of preoccupation with self and self-advantage we are committed to affirm the essential conviction that all life is from God and is of God and that all our living and loving has to be a share in God's continuing creation. When others who marry and beget children may understandably grow weary, disillusioned and cynical, we, the single-minded, have to be free to say: 'No, you were right in the first place; you were right when you loved; you were right when you rejoiced in the birth of your child; you are right now if you go on to live and to love anew.'

17: Commitment

Until the peaceful revolution of 1989 visitors to Communist countries often expressed surprise that churches were open and crowded with worshippers. It was taken to mean that religion was thriving and enjoyed State tolerance if not approval and support. Of course if religion were nothing more than going to church on Sundays and feastdays, if it were no more than a personal, individual activity that does not spill over into, and radically affect, the events of daily life and the conduct of the community and the State, then Communism was grudgingly prepared to coexist with religion. It feared no harm from that kind of privatised and spiritualised religion, and with ample reason. A faith that comes to life only within the walls of a church, that is allowed no schools, newspapers, access to the media, groups, meetings or activities, a faith whose priests are confined to the altar and the sacristy, is essentially a faith in chains, emasculated and tamed. Communism, after failing to crush the Churches by brutal persecution, was prepared to sit it out and watch them diminish and die, deprived of the oxygen of freedom. It made a huge miscalculation because it never understood that the religious instinct, however repressed, continues to germinate and regenerate itself in the human heart.

The situation here, of course, is quite different but just as dangerous for the cause of faith and Christian commitment. We are free to breathe but often only polluted air. We are free, but lack the energy, determination and commitment to take up the challenge of freedom. Without external pressures, we have become, from a variety of causes, little better than 'closet-Christians'. With no burning inner conviction or passion for the values of God's kingdom on earth and with a spiritual diffidence that borders on timidity, we are perceived to be safe, decent, acceptable and agreeable people. Catholics, for instance, pose such a feeble challenge to society that it seems quite ludicrous that Ian Paisley or the Wee Frees should still consider us evil, dangerous and diabolical people. The raging fire of Pentecost now merely glows amid the embers and ashes, deprived of the oxygen of passionate conviction.

We need to ask ourselves how much our Christian faith and Catholic commitment mean to us. The acid test is sacrifice. What is more precious to us? What would we – or do we – choose in preference to our faith, our God, our Church? Faced with a choice like Dr Faust, for what would we sell our soul? For love, money, fame, a quiet life? How much time, attention and energy are we ready to devote to the following of Jesus Christ and to the coming of his kingdom on earth? If we have ever encountered the living God and experienced the awesome and enchanting reality of God's presence in Christ, then we remain God-haunted for the rest of our lives, restless till we possess him. There is no room here for the cool and the calculating. The overwhelming excitement never leaves us and drives us on to explore ever more deeply the mystery that is God and the wonder of his life and love. It is an experience that changes and transforms us. Religion is so much more than moral decency, or a taste for ritual and the rarefied delights of personal prayer or dignified liturgy. It has to do with life itself. Without it we remain among the living dead.

Religion in Britain has become overpoweringly respectable. It is regarded as an acceptable private preoccupation. It is embraced if at all with a remarkable degree of moderation and restraint. Our religious leaders would have nothing in common with the shaggy, desert-hardened prophets of old, the unpredictable and untameable Elijah and his disciple Elisha. In the New Testament, too, Christ numbered among his disciples men as nasty and crass as James and John the sons of Zebedee. He was approached on occasions by those who would follow him but only on clearly specified terms. Jesus gave them short shrift. They had to choose between family responsibilities and the single-minded following of the Son of Man who had nowhere to lay his head. Disciples should let the dead bury their dead, never look back once their hand is laid on the plough, be ready to sell everything, give to the poor and follow him in total freedom. His point was always sharp and uncompromising. Both in the Old Testament and the New, God's work has to be done by real flesh and blood people like us with their own ideas and approach. Some of us know what should be done to put the world to rights. Like the sons of Zebedee we would smite the unworthy and the unwelcoming; we would wipe out and destroy our enemies or the enemies of God as we see them. But the Word of God shows us that the real enemy, the blockage, is within our very selves. If the kingdom is to come we have to get our own priorities right. We cannot be followers of Christ's way of life unless we are prepared to abandon our neurotic need for security and follow where the Spirit leads. We cannot find life unless we are brave enough to live in the present and for the present, putting the past to rest and letting things be. We cannot go forward unless we are free from the pressures of conformity. We should not be looking to others for approval. We are to make the world a more fruitful place in our own way and out of the fullness of our own hearts in the here and now.

18: Learning the Samaritan Way

It simply is not true to say that we are living in a permissive age. The same people who will be broad-minded and liberal about sex and drugs are likely to be fiercely moralistic about smoking, high-fibre diets and jogging. Revolutionaries and the left wing generally can be violently authoritarian in denying speech to right-wing opponents. We all maintain values which for us are sacred and non-negotiable; we choose our morality and then defend or impose it with determination. As human beings we retain a sense of right and wrong but we are in an unusual situation. Values and beliefs are shifting. There is little or no common ground. The moral confusion that ensues is deeply disturbing and tends to pull apart the fabric of our society. If we cannot agree on what is right and wrong, it is difficult to uphold a system of law. There is no consensus, no shared values. This is bad for society and bad too for individuals. Young people growing up in the midst of such confusion are virtually thrown on their own resources and tend to accept or reject standards according to prevailing fashion or their limited experience and that of their peers.

Yet it is clearly important to establish what is right and wrong and to discover convincing reasons for such choices. Mere sentiment, custom or appeal to authority are insufficient. When under pressure, values are not underpinned by any consistent logic and social consensus. They cannot hold fast.

People seem often to imagine that traditional notions of right and wrong are quite arbitrarily laid down by the Christian Church which is now seen by many to be out of date and repressive. Many too believe they can pick and choose what suits them or fits their preferred life-style. They dine à la carte rather than table d'hôte. They do not realise that Christian morality and moral values derive from a coherent and integrated vision of life. It is a way of looking at life and death which is based on the insights and teachings of the Jewish Law and Prophets and the supreme wisdom of Jesus Christ. It has then been further elaborated by the experience and reflection of believers who for 2,000 years have been faithfully following the Christian way. Yet the Word of God tells us that guidance and fulfilment can also be found close at hand – by knowing ourselves better, by realising who we are and what we are made for, by following through the consequences of our Christian beliefs. The Christian stance, however, is a lot more radical and demanding than most people realise.

We can see a particular instance of this in the familiar story of the Samaritan on the Jericho road. The parable has passed into our language and culture, but its freshness and force can be appreciated every time it is read. It is a specific application of the wider principle that if we want to get our values straight we must put God first, focus on him with all the force, intensity and love that we can muster and then commit ourselves to the service and best interests of others. Concern and practical care should not be confined to our relatives, friends and fellow citizens, our natural allies, but should embrace the whole of humanity without distinction. One and the selfsame love has to be lavished without distinction on friend and enemy alike, near and far, the ill-favoured as well as the attractive, the worthless as well as the worthwhile, the rejected and despised as well as the respectable and well-regarded. This is a hard saying, a near-impossible demand. What Christ and our religion say is that anything less than this degrades and demeans the new humanity we can share since Christ gave us the radical new option. Reconciliation, love, rebuilding community and human solidarity make for a better world and a better people. It is a gradual transformation of individuals and society that is brought into being by the unchurched as well as by believers. In fact it is often the Samaritan who sets the pace. With such a vision, the precepts and demands of the Bible and especially of the New Testament gain coherence, force, intelligibility. It is far more than a simple matter of being kind to the unfortunate.

If we want to know the real reason behind it all, if we want to gasp at the sweep and beauty of the total vision then it is useful to follow the prompting of the Church's Sunday Lectionary (15th Sunday of the Year [Cycle C]) and link the Samaritan story with reflection on St Paul's letter to the Colossians (1:15–20). Paul's ideas may seem remote from daily Christian living but they help to create the necessary context in which to understand the more familiar story of the Samaritan.

St Paul teaches that the whole world, the entire universe, all material things, every human person, are brought into being as an expression of God, of God's being, his beauty, his truth. Everything, by being truly itself, leads us closer to the knowledge and the very reality of God. Nothing lies outside the life and mystery of God. All is made in the Word, is brought into being by the Word, is patterned on the Word. Everything, therefore, including ourselves, is loved by the Father as he loves the Son his Word in the Holy Spirit. We who want to be fully and consciously ourselves have to see ourselves consciously as part of God's creation but primarily as part of the mystery of God. We are known and loved by the Father in the Son. God recognises in us an expression, finite and fragmented, of his own self. When we know and love him we relate to him who is all in all. And we can only know and love because God's Spirit, his very self, is within us and has made its home in us. The Christian vision reveals to us that we are truly divine when most fully human. And we are loved not for what we do but for what we are. We can never be lost to God.

To realise this is freedom. We come truly alive and fully human when we see all reality as God sees it, when we love all reality as God loves it. This state of mind, this attitude to life, has practical consequences in so many ways. It determines how we approach freedom, friendship, human rights, animal welfare, ecology, the pursuit of wealth, racial equality, anything and everything. It is the innermost secret of life; it is our precious gift from Christ, true God, true man, and eternal Word. Because of this profound vision we have to be stewards and attentive guardians of all that exists. We should be Samaritans to our neighbours, not just out of pity but because we come from God and are of God. Our intelligence and love, godlike energies, are meant to heal and unite, not to exploit, dominate and divide.

19: The Consequences of Love

Adolf Hitler was born in April 1889. The occasion of his centenary prompted a couple of television documentaries and a certain amount of press coverage. The dreadful images of the recent past returned to haunt and accuse not just the German people but humanity as well. Josef Stalin, throughout roughly the same period, caused comparable oppression, bloodshed and human degradation. Together they created living hells in the name of the new world order: a Third Reich that would last a thousand years, a Workers' State that would finally liberate the labouring masses. Both dictators were ruthless in the pursuit of their phantasies. They were indifferent to human suffering and obsessed with the need to secure the supremacy of their system, their race, their class. Both helped to determine the history of our time. They must not be forgotten or ignored.

The Word of God insists always that we love each other as Christ loves us. It is important then that we try to understand what it really means to be a Christian, to be part of a new creation and citizens of an alternative society. Hitler and Stalin stand for the worship of power, conflict, domination; they were dealers in death. They are a hideous reminder of what human beings can inflict on each other. The Gospel of Jesus Christ invites us to a radically different life-style and alternative values. If his followers, the Christians of the twentieth century, had really listened and taken that teaching to heart, the Third Reich and the Communist revolution would have been stillborn. Yet even today, after the bloody lessons of this century, we fail dismally to draw on our Christian faith to shape our society, to determine our political, social and economic goals. Desperately schizophrenic, we privatise our religion, making it almost entirely a matter of personal salvation, while in daily life we, in practice, worship other gods and serve other masters. We are not evil or obsessed like Hitler or Stalin but neither are we a sign of hope, a positive force on the side of life and love. On the whole we prefer to be passive and private; decent but conformist; unwilling to stand out, stand up and suffer for a cause.

In 1979 I stood for hours within the barbed wire fences of Auschwitz, surely the ultimate symbol of evil. I was present when the first Polish pope returned home. Surrounded by the ruins of a society without God, I vowed then that I would never cease to oppose and if necessary to fight anything in life, from State or Church or any power bloc, that degraded, manipulated or exploited any human being for whatever cause. To do so in the name of any objective whatever sins against the light of the Gospel. In the past, and in our own day too, Church and State have sometimes excused personal and private cruelty in the name of a greater good. It is imperative that we never fall into that trap for we have all – too tragically – gone down that path before. We must never drink from the poisoned chalice but seek instead the pure waters of life from Christ himself.

Any time we come to church and share in the Church's worship, we are making a statement and not just fulfilling a religious obligation. We stake our present and future on the reality of the living God. He is our God, we are his people. We are supposed to be committed to the overwhelming truth that a whole new world order came into being with Christ and we are part of it. Christ brought into human history a new, all-consuming passion. He embodied the absolute, unconditional love of the Creator God for each and every created thing, for each individual but also for the whole of our world and the cosmos of which it is part. He then says calmly and without qualification: you are to love as I love. Immediately the shackles of our selfishness have to be cast aside, our blind eyes opened, our hearts of stone made hearts of flesh. We have to become other Christs. Like

him we undoubtedly will be misunderstood, ridiculed and
rejected by our own as well as by others as we live out in
practice the terrifying consequences of love. But that is what
following Christ really means.

20:   Human Suffering

I read somewhere that Winston Churchill once remarked that success is never final and failure never fatal. Yet when we are young, pain, rejection, failure and loss can loom so large in our life that it can block out the daylight and leave us feeling utterly desperate and sometimes suicidal. When we get older and perhaps more mature, the objective pain and distress can be greater but there is greater endurance, more perspective and wider experience. We can bear the pain. Then as bodily powers begin to dwindle, depression and defeat can leave us exhausted and blank. But at all stages in life we have to accept the reality of pain and suffering. It is a fond and foolish phantasy to dream of a peaceful haven, an oasis from which can be banished the normal upsets and trials of life. Evil, cruelty, suffering are to be with us to the end of time; they are part of the mystery of human existence. It seems inevitable and even, in a strange way, desirable that progress and growth should be accompanied by struggle and tension and sacrifice. They are as necessary as success and smoothness. They challenge us to produce from our inner resources the very best that is in us. That is why human beings are given powers of determination, goodness, resilience and courage. Without pain and suffering they would never need to be called upon. It would be an undemanding, stagnant and complacent world and an inhuman existence.

Jesus Christ had no illusions about the future that awaited him. He was always clear-eyed. He foresaw the consequences of his words and actions. He was fully aware that his message spelled the ultimate defeat of institutionalised oppression and injustice. The Good News was intended to liberate men and women here and now from their chains whether these were psychological, religious or political. He knew that the men of power would react with savagery and determination to block his influence and wipe out his words. They would hunt him down and silence him by any means at their disposal. He saw ahead the way of pain and suffering. It was the price to be paid. He must have dreaded it but he never flinched. He was to drain the cup of human experience to the dregs. In defeat he would know victory; and through death win life everlasting.

Those of us who profess to be Christian, who are trying to walk his way, would be foolish to imagine that a life of service, of unconditional love, can be pursued painlessly and prosperously. We shall be misunderstood, exploited, ridiculed – as he was. When we choose this path it is not for the sake of profit. We strike no bargains with God. We do not of course seek out suffering. We have to be prepared, however, for the sake of the kingdom to do what we have to do even if it involves pain and rejection and the carrying of the cross. We too are part of the mystery of evil. We find life by outfacing death.

We are no braver, no nobler than others so what makes it possible for us to follow Christ – if in fact we are ready to do so? It depends as always on our vision and our understanding of life. It helps us to carry on if we have a glimmer of understanding of what the suffering is really about.

We have to visualise all human history as one continuous outpouring of God's creative love. Human minds, energies and skills have to wrestle with reality, fashioning and utilising resources constantly to create our world. There is the power of human love to embrace, heal, reconcile others. There is the gift of human intellect to penetrate, analyse, categorise, to explore all that exists. And all this ceaseless, creative enterprise of the human spirit is being undertaken in Christ to enable all that is created to find its fulfilment and purpose in him, and then through him to return to the Father. None of this can happen without coming into direct conflict with the powers of darkness, chaos and division. That causes pain but the struggle must go on. We have to be willing to accept pain and sometimes apparent defeat since we are assured that all will be well and all manner of things will be well. We are convinced that, beneath all, is the overflowing underground river of God's love and being: it can never be dammed nor stopped. We meet him in darkness as well as in light; in pain as well as in joy. It is reason enough for us to be ready to suffer, to be tested even to destruction and, if need be, to die. There is a richer reality than our personal happiness and freedom from pain. There is a more basic imperative, a fundamental option of light or darkness. We make our choice . . . and must be ready to pay the price.

21: Living Water

I have a theory about the Gospel story of the woman by the well. I used to wonder why we have this remarkably detailed account of what was a private conversation between Jesus and the Samaritan woman. He must have taken great pains to tell the whole story to his disciples. Partly, I imagine, because of the immense significance of what passed between them but also, I suspect, to fend off the scandalised reproaches of his followers. What was he thinking of, talking to a woman alone by a well? A Samaritan, too, an outcast and from a despised minority. Could he not see what sort of woman she was? The sort that can't resist a man. Five times married and now living in sin. It could cost a man his reputation just talking to the likes of her. I can picture Christ having to tell the whole story and tell it more than once to reassure the prudes and the prurient among his followers. Gently but firmly he would have to repeat that the point was not about sin but about new life. His encounter had nothing to do with condemnation and throwing the first stone at the sinner but with thirst for God and springs of living water. In the new kingdom everyone comes in on the same footing, with the same gift, the same chance of life and love unending. Their past is dead, buried and forgotten.

Year by year we are given the time of Lent as essentially an opportunity for preparation, for ploughing and sowing. Easter lies ahead, the festival of life, liberation, baptism and resurrection. The freshness and vitality of Easter is summed up in the symbol of water. Yet it is important to realise that water does not merely clean but is essentially the water of life. It quenches our thirst, keeps us alive, gives drink to the beasts and enables crops to grow.

When Jesus encountered the all-too-human woman by the well he reacted as he always seemed to do in the presence of human frailty and sinfulness. He allowed himself, as it were, to be handicapped. Here was a woman like this and no canon lawyer available to unravel the legal tangle, no marriage counsellor or psychiatrist to help the client accept her sexuality, no preacher to scourge her for her promiscuity! Instead the Son of God and son of man seemed to treat forgiveness as the norm and the sin as a symptom not a scandal. He does not prescribe penances, cold showers, moral rehabilitation. He tries instead to open sinful eyes to a new kingdom and a new way of living. Once we can see the secret of our own selves, the marvellous heights and depths open to anyone born of God as his child, then we know without any other telling what we have to do. We then instinctively grasp how we should live in a world made beautiful by the love of God and his abiding presence. Anyone can enjoy this new way of life whether it be a religious fanatic like Paul, a rough, tough fisherman like Peter, a prostitute like Magdalene or the village slut from Samaria. Since everything is the gift of God and is offered by him with the same passionate love to everyone, anyone can wake up, leave the ways of death and walk the paths of real life. It is on offer to all who are prepared to worship in spirit and in truth.

This has much that is salutary to say to each of us. We are often tempted to sneak a look at our balance-sheet and to claim credit for the good things but to excuse the bad. We prefer to forget that of ourselves we are nothing, and have nothing to boast of in God's sight. He loves us regardless. We each exist and have a future because from eternity he has liked the idea of us. That is the confidence we can cling to in the desert of our daily lives, in dryness and desolation. He loves us and goes on loving us. In fact he can do no other. We have to believe it. And if we do believe it, if we see his love in all that happens, in everything that surrounds us, in the depths of our own selves, then we can always find reason to live. There is always meaning and a hope to live for. An inner peace wells up within us without end. We have found the eternal spring of living water.

22: The Way of Life

Most of us whether happy or depressed, successful or defeated, fail to break free from the chains of self-regard. We
always keep ourselves to the forefront; we are effectively
the centre of all creation. Everything in heaven and earth
is evaluated in relationship to myself and my needs. Even
God and the supernatural are enlisted in the service of
myself. Obedience and belief are conceded conditionally.
It all depends upon whether God measures up to my ideas
and safeguards my interests and those of the people closest
to me. The whole world, with its past, its present and future,
is effectively scaled down to my narrow horizons and my
personal standpoint. Even if I am inclined to be religious,
the whole point is seen to be my individual salvation,
my own eternal happiness. I can never cut loose from
myself. I am still the substitute God, the ultimate value.
Even if I am full of self-disgust, it is myself that looms
largest in my landscape. And all of that is still the way
of death. It is a distortion which is the consequence of
sin and the penalty of pride.

Jesus Christ shows us another way, a fuller life and a richer
truth. First and foremost, he offers a new attitude and a
more realistic view of reality. The self-centred perception is
as out of date and mistaken as the belief that the earth is flat
and the centre of the universe. Once we broke through to
a better knowledge of things as they are, we have been
able to make increasing sense of our planet, its place in
the scheme of things and the possibilities of growth and
development. The same is true of our personal attitudes. A
changed perception can transform my attitudes and values.

The world does not belong to me; I belong to the world. I am part of it and have responsibility to it and to others. I am but a link in the chain and a drop in the ocean. I am of absolute value and worth but essentially as part, not whole. To embrace that viewpoint, to absorb it into the marrow of my being, is a kind of personal death but is the start of new and endless life. It transforms the quality of one's life. I let go the fanciful and the transitory. I begin to sink into the eternal and the divine within myself. I let God be in myself and in others.

And from that moment on, life then becomes increasingly fresh and renewed. True faith in God and real religion are not for spiritual geriatrics and the nostalgic. They centre on God who is the ever-creative, the ever-new. That is why God is revealed in Jesus Christ as being the God of forgiveness and the fresh start. It is not just because God is kindly and merciful, but it is because in him there can be no death and no ultimate frustration. Sin and the wilful wanderings of human pride hinder his sharing of himself and prevent me from enjoying to the full the blessings of life and love. He, though, never stops seeking ways to heal, restore and renew. He does not wait for me, but woos me, warming me back into a life which is more rational and loving. In that sense, he is not interested in the past and does not want me to dwell in the past or on the past. What matters is his being *now*, my being *now* in union with him, in conscious, loving identity with the rest of the world, the whole of God's universe. I have to be constantly in search of what is life-giving and be prepared to live and work for it.

We continue to live in a fallen, failed world only because we approach it and visualise it to be fallen and failed and in so far as we refuse to believe in the redemption. We are in fact living, and meant to be living, in a reconciled and wholesome world. We can only enter it and make it happen if we are prepared to take Christ at his word and to realise that in him we are made a new creation. We are no longer children of the old Adam, but children of the living God, brothers and sisters of Christ. Forgiven ourselves, forgiving others, we should be ready and able to take up every challenge of life.

It is that faith which gives freedom, inner peace and stronger purpose.

A YEAR IN THE LIFE OF . . .

Introduction

A believer should be ready to see God in all creation and in all human experience. At the heart of things is always the sacred. We need to be constantly aware of that presence and be open to the Spirit. We need also to listen intently to what the world is saying, for that reveals God too. There is an endless variety of pathways to God but they all have a starting-point in our human condition, our shared experience of life, its joys and sadness, its hopes and fears. We must be ready to explore, not determined to compel people along tramlines to a predictable conclusion, however worthy. A booklet in the present Decade of Evangelisation puts it this way: 'Our first task in approaching another people, another culture, another religion, is to take off our shoes, for the place we are approaching is holy. Else we may find ourselves treading on another's dream. More serious still we may forget that God was there before our arrival.'

It is a fundamental criticism of much religious activity and attitudes that even now faith is rarely incarnational, and frequently fails to take the world and its peoples seriously. We tend to lecture and even to hector what we subconsciously regard as the opposition without pausing to stand in respectful silence and to listen to what is being communicated. It stems perhaps from a traditional distrust of the world and its ways and from failing to attach importance to the transient and the created.

To make sense of the passing scene and of our lives we need always to remind ourselves that Jesus Christ is the Word of God. As such, he is quite simply the pattern and blueprint of creation. By what he is, he reveals to us the fundamental grammar and thought patterns of God the creator. He contains in himself the logic of all life and existence. When Jesus Christ teaches us how to look at life and death, his insights are not optional good advice; they cut to the very heart of things. His life equally is a statement of truth about reality. His death and resurrection, the very point of his becoming man, are the answer to the riddle of existence. Death and resurrection are the key to the mystery of all being. They unlock all the doors.

Death and rebirth, Calvary and the Easter Garden, are the biorhythm of all reality. There is a clear correlation between the seasons of the year and the Church's liturgical celebration. The Christian story is not a mythical and mystical presentation of nature's cycle. The seasons instead should be recognised as an echo in nature of the divine dynamic. Humanity too shares in the same process. To become fully human, to grow to full stature as a person it is necessary to respond to this biorhythm; to live by dying, to possess by letting go, to enjoy by renunciation of ownership. Jesus Christ demands of us a recycling of behaviour that might appear to involve a death but which is in fact a resurrection and new life. Happiness is to be found not in the pursuit of pleasure but in awareness and acceptance of the basic laws of all reality and life.

Awareness here is crucial. Any true spirituality must be informed and inspired by an awakening and a new awareness. The things of God around and within us are not discovered and possessed in a rarefied atmosphere of the unworldly and intangible. When our blind eyes see, the presence of God around and within us is revealed and we are enfolded in the everlasting arms.

1: Advent

It would be amusing if it were not so harmful to see the difference there is between the real Christian we are called to be and the caricature Christian that so many people criticise and reject. The caricature Christian is supposed to be a middle-aged or elderly fuddy-duddy, clinging romantically and nostalgically to the past, remote from life, generally disapproving of sex and the world, so heavenly minded as to be no earthly use. Out of touch, out of date, a relic of the past. But the truth is that the real Christian is not a person of the past at all, but of the present and the future. We are meant to be Advent people, committed to the Coming, to a world that is being continuously remade and demands of us every scrap of our energy, idealism, sense of values and intelligence. Whatever our biological age, true Christians have to be young in heart, alert and alive to every development and sign of growth in our world, persons of hope and undimmed faith, who see God's presence and purposes here and now, in all that happens in this living world, this throbbing universe.

In Advent the Church rejoices in its own New Year. It looks to the Coming, to the transformation of ourselves and our world. That is why it has special meaning for the young who have no fear of change, since for them all is new and exciting. The rest of us, with scar tissue to show for our bruising past, need to pray for the inflooding energy of the Holy Spirit to encourage us to a realisation that change is always possible, that God is the great underground river that no one can dam up and no one can stop. As Carlo Carretto says: 'Creativity is God's, collaboration is ours.

The call is God's. The reply is ours.' Young and old alike have a part to play in building the kingdom of God within our very selves, in society, in our cities and towns. It is not our project but God's. We respond; we do not initiate. We are, each of us, whether old or young, called by God to an obedience which is free and ennobling. We are to let God work through our minds, hearts and hands to achieve his purposes for the world he is constantly creating.

God is intent on transforming all things. He wants first and foremost to become more alive and evident in ourselves and in our relationships. The Christ Child in Bethlehem can be seen as a seed of life, the divine leaven which must, through us and our own transformation, reshape the whole of creation. The importance of Christmas is that it has to happen in us, our lives, our communities.

We have to become aware of what that might mean for us. God wants to change us by coming more and more into our life, thoughts, decisions. He is already the real if unacknowledged source of life, gifts, energy. He wants each of us to become ever more alive to his presence and his touch. We need to give a more conscious and free assent to that image and likeness of himself which is our real self, our true inner identity. We are so often, and for so much of the time, self-seeking and selfish, dealing in the ways of death. We are broken, hurtful and destructive. We need silence, honesty and deep centring prayer to encounter our true self and to be God's presence to others. It is a growth that takes a lifetime.

And then, aware of God in ourselves, we have to be able to see God's image in others. An American professor on his retirement was asked the secret of his incredible personal influence on others. He said simply: 'I see the image of God in them and I adore it.' That expresses the reverence and the love we should develop for others. That can gradually and sometimes painfully change all our relationships. God can then come into our living and loving almost tangibly. We find that a difficult process. We find God blocked by our perceptions and judgemental reactions. We have to open ourselves constantly to the love, life and light of God.

Changed dynamically in ourselves and in our personal relationships we can then become a seed of life, a sign of peace, a light in the darkness in all our dealings in business, work, family, politics and society. Little is ever changed by diktat from above. True transformation has to be vital and total, from the good earth up. We can each be part of that process. God manifests his goodness, life and creativity in endless, unstoppable ways. If we are sensitive and alive enough to take notice we can encourage and make ourselves part of every initiative for good, for healing and for renewal. God does not work only through the Churches. We do God's work not only in church and doing churchy things but every time we apply our minds, talents and energies to making things work, to serving and supplying others' needs, to upholding justice, true humanity and authentic human values. Jesus lived and laboured in the obscurity and daily round of Nazareth for some thirty years before the brief, spectacular time of his public ministry. But at all times he was effectively fulfilling the will of his Father and the work of our redemption.

2: Advent Again

It is so rare to get what you want for Christmas that a long time ago I decided I would give myself every year the present I really felt I needed. It has not been an unqualified success: the thing you set your heart on rarely turns out to be all you had expected. I remember Cardinal Hume one day writing about the shrine of Our Lady outside Freiburg in Switzerland. Among the thanksgiving plaques in the shrine is one which reads: Thank you for not granting my request. Our needs are so confused; our dreams so fanciful; our priorities so dimly perceived that it is not surprising we remain in a state of dissatisfaction and suffering from a kind of aimlessness. We are always waiting for something fulfilling, something that will change us and our whole situation. The mistake is that we think it can come from outside.

The weeks leading up to Christmas are in the commercial world a kind of fantasy. It is tinsel time. There is an artificially created feverishness to make us forgetful of the dark and the cold, a secular promise of happier tomorrows. Advent means simply the Coming. It does not mean pretending that Bethlehem will be repeated year by year but it does remind us that God who came to birth in Bethlehem as the son of Mary is now constantly coming to birth in our history, in all humanity and in ourselves. We now live in a time which is a permanent, perpetual Advent. If we had but eyes to see and ears to hear we would be able to recognise that here is our God. God is being made manifest in us, in our lives, in history, in all that is. He is perpetually coming to birth in us so that we, other Christs, make holy all we touch and offer it back to the Father in a constant sacrifice of prayer and praise and thanksgiving. Christmas has to be happening inside each one of us. We need to become alive to it.

It is very important to realise that we are blessed beyond words in the glory of our calling. All the images of peace, overflowing integrity, of blessing and abundance that we read of in the prophets and the Advent liturgies are now coming to pass in these last days. Since the coming of Christ we have entered a decisive and quite magnificent era, 'the latter days', the ultimate stage of growth and transformation. We miss so much because we are not always looking in the right places. The new heavens and the new earth are being shaped all around us through the ingenuity, technological genius and scientific knowledge of the human race. God's life and love are evident everywhere and in everything. They are not confined to the Church nor exclusively to its activity. Whenever humanity moves forward, God's revelation is being fulfilled. Sacred and secular are not two realities but a single expression of the one God. We can rejoice in the bewildering profusion of goods and opportunities on offer to us today. We are making enormous strides in the harnessing of the world's potential. The human race too is being urged into great unity, solidarity, awareness, a more vivid sense of justice and equality. At the same time there remains sin, the option for the illusory self, the shadow not the reality, an emptiness that cries out for God. There is still the valley of the shadow of death. Yet we are made for light, life and love, for the living God. We are on the way; God too comes to meet us. We yearn for what we are not yet; in the dark of each December we dream of the light. We are nothing, yet we are called to be immortal; we are in search of the Godhead which is our only true fulfilment. We must begin to explore the mystery of God where, as was revealed to Mother Julian of Norwich, 'in life is wondrous familiarity, and in love is gentle courtesy and in light is endless kindness' (*A Lesson of Love: The Revelations of Julian of Norwich*, p. 209).

3: Christmas Time

By December 14 each year I suffer from an overdose of
Christmas. I experience moments of undiluted panic because
I have not sent a single Christmas card or bought a solitary
present. I have friends who buy next year's cards from
left-over stock in January, and who have all their presents
gift-wrapped by September. Most of us feel some kind of
guilt because we are beset by advertising and promotion
that place impossible demands on us as consumers and on
the celebration of an event in which so few really believe.
It is little wonder then that, under the weight of all this
commercial anticipation, Christmas has changed its identity
and has become a week-long (or even a fortnight-long)
break from the gloom of winter.

The substitute Christmas places almost exclusive empha-
sis on food, drink, conviviality. It stresses that Christmas
is the time for getting and giving gifts. It shuts out the
harshness and pain of the everyday world and invites us
into fantasy. All of this is a faint echo of the full-blooded
rejoicing of the Catholic world in centuries past which we
can glimpse in the carols and customs of Merrie England. At
the time of the Reformation Puritans and Roundheads tried
to abolish Christmas in their distaste for sinful humanity
and the pleasures of the flesh. The Catholic instinct has
been to avoid both extremes, extravagant self-indulgence
or grim-faced austerity. Gift-giving, light-hearted rejoicing,
a reaching out to family, friends and to the hard-pressed and
forgotten, all these are part of a genuine Christmas. They are
rooted in the reality of what happened in Bethlehem nearly
2,000 years ago.

When we celebrate the birth of the child who was God we are not simply looking backward, dwelling on a vanished world of innocence. Our celebration, in sacrament, song and festivity, makes real in our lives the living presence of that same Christ Child. It makes it possible for us to be healed, affirmed and enriched by him. It helps us to go on trying to make the kingdom of God a bit more real in our world. Our celebration of Christmas, while summoning up the past, is totally engaged in the here and now; and looks forward in joy and hope to what is yet to be. At the time of Christmas we are saying to others: yes, this time is good; yes, there is hope for us all, there is meaning in all our striving; yes, we are loved and can love; yes, there is a promise of life ahead that will grow richer and never end. It is not because we are prosperous, healthy or because, as they say, we have it made. It is not because we are having a great time now. It is simply and solely because something has happened which has changed the face of life, altered human history, given new purpose and meaning to everything. At a particular moment in time, in a hill village in Judaea, in the outbuildings of a caravanserai, to a mother uprooted from home at the diktat of the Roman Emperor, a child was born. He united in himself, uniquely, the human and the divine. He was, by human descent, heir to King David and yet Son of the everlasting Father: Jesus Christ, true man, true God.

And what does that event so long ago mean for us now and for our future? We can go on exploring the consequences without ever coming to the end.

The coming to birth of a child who was Son of God gives a new value and worth to every human life. After the birth of Jesus we must think of every human being as brother or sister of that child who was God. Even the poorest, most deprived, most pathetic scrap of humanity is infinitely precious since God took to himself our human nature. The birth of Jesus Christ establishes the foundation for absolute human equality. The consequence of that is that we have to become resolute against racism and discrimination of every kind. That has to become a Christian passion and not just the obsession of the liberal.

Since God became flesh and blood, living, loving, feeling, dreaming, relating like the rest of us, all material things have taken on a new loveliness. Their natural worth has been enhanced and transfigured by the living presence of God within. The consequence for a Christian is that the material world is not to be despised or feared. Its beauty is not a snare but part of God's revealing of himself. Our flesh and blood, our hopes and dreams, our loving and relationships, our eating, drinking, delighting in life and its richness, all of these things are sealed and affirmed by the presence and the involvement of God in his, and our, shared reality. We can now see things as they are, treasure them as gifts of God and glimpses of him, offer them back to him with heartfelt thanksgiving and wondering respect. That is the way to be at peace with all things and to rejoice in the reality of redemption.

As we reflect on the Christ Child, we can sense something of the wonder of a love that can give itself so humbly, so totally, so generously to the beloved. Our instinct to give gifts at Christmas is an echo of that original self-giving of God to his creatures. We know too that the gift of the Christ Child will never be revoked. It began a new era of divine self-giving, carried through by the presence and the power of the Holy Spirit in our world. The Holy Spirit showers gifts on all of us, gives life and love to us every moment of our lives and makes every day a kind of Christmas. We rejoice in that daily loving. We give thanks for that divine generosity. We recognise the power of the Spirit at work in our lives and in others; we give gifts to others because we try to love as we are loved. We want to be part of the same outpouring of goodness and affirmation on to the world we rejoice in. That is Christmas; it is our vocation and daily joy as Christians.

4: Christmas Cheer

Only seven per cent of adults in Britain believe the celebration of Christ's birth to be the important point of Christmas. That was the stark fact in a survey published in December 1988.

God first stole into his world so secretly and silently that his coming was known only to desperately poor herdsmen on the hillside outside Bethlehem and to a handful of wise men whose ancient and secret knowledge of the planets led them to believe that a king had been born in Israel. His stealth has persisted to this day; he is silently subversive. There is a mixture in the Christmas story of the instantly recognisable and the eternal, remote and utterly mysterious. We are dealing here with no pretty fairytale that crumbles when exposed to analysis. This is the decisive act of all human history. Something happened that demands we stretch our minds and open our hearts.

Hereafter there is always to be a new dimension. Men and women everywhere, in every culture and at all times, have the assurance that creation has a single source, a single purpose and a meaning. All things are intelligible, and so can be understood, harnessed and developed. All things have as their inmost source of energy and dynamism an eternal and unceasing force which is benevolent, life-giving and positive. We call it love; we call it God. The bedrock of our certainty is our faith that this God became man in Jesus Christ. The coming of Christ into human history has unleashed all the divine forces of creativity and intelligence that in fact have shaped our modern world and that open up for us endless perspectives of future progress. Our world is revealed in Christ as essentially and ultimately intelligible and friendly; our humanity as capable of endless transformation and growth. All this springs from a birth in a stable at Bethlehem, a secret and ignored birth, but ultimately the one that remains eternally significant.

It is hard to link this with a walk among the jostling crowds on the High Street, the clamour of the voices demanding our attention and our money, the parties and the presents that make up our modern Christmas. Rather than reject all that, I prefer to enjoy it as the consequence of that birth so long ago, to see the commercial Christmas as a distorted echo of the original message, the Good News proclaimed to the world from Bethlehem. There is light and colour in winter darkness, jollity and friendliness in a suspicious and divided world, generosity and gift-giving in a selfish, self-centred society. All this echoes, even if it distorts, a surprising and subversive fact of life. From Bethlehem onwards God is committed to our planet and our history, in a special and specifically human way. The stable at Bethlehem represents faith in a humanity now made one with divinity. It unites the weak and the wise and makes them witness to this new humanity. It makes clear that from the grass-roots all human activity is now endowed with divine purpose and beauty. This is the true light in winter darkness; this is the hope and joy that is to be found in interdependence and solidarity; this is the reason for recognising and rejoicing in that fellowship and friendship which is to be found each Christmas because we can look at a human child and adore a divine Saviour.

The consequence of that birth so long ago is that each subsequent birth also becomes significant, because it brings into the world a new life destined for God and makes each one of us truly a child of God and heir to the kingdom and its maker. Nothing now depends ultimately upon secular rank and privilege; all is given freely to every son and daughter of God called into life by the Father. There is now no room for mutual hostility nor icy indifference. The redeemer has become our peace. There is now possible a new understanding, a new imperative that will, throughout history, reshape structures and go on doing so until reconciled humanity can live in freedom and mutual respect. Bethlehem really has changed the world and all our future.

Is all this Utopian? Hopeless idealism? I prefer to see it rather as the coming of the kingdom of God into the city of man, a seed of glory. It is a source of hope and a vision to shape the future. No wonder that the unborn John the Baptist leaps in Elizabeth's womb. The human race has been given in the birth of Jesus Christ the secret of endless life and ceaseless progress. That is why I have learned to celebrate rather than condemn, embrace rather than reject, give thanks in prayer rather than bewail past failures.

5:   New Year

You would have thought that experience might have made us wary of welcoming the New Year. The passage of time leaves us richer in experience but much more weather-beaten in the process. Yet the parties and the revelry that greet the New Year are clearly signs of a human instinct to rejoice in the present and to look with anticipation to the future. In a sense, we can experience each new day as a fresh start. Ring out the old, ring in the new.

Like a lot of other people, each New Year, we reminisce about the past, lament the passing of loved ones, the golden years, wish perhaps that it were possible to turn back the clock, to recover lost certainties and vanished values. As in most other things and at most other times, we are a tangle of mixed emotions.

If asked, I suppose most people would regard religion as a stabilising influence in the midst of confusion and change, as part of the cherished past rather than as something dynamic, thrusting, revolutionary. It is seen as a refuge, an oasis, cosy and reassuring but unreal. That is perhaps how most would regard the Church and its message at Christmas and each New Year.

Yet the Word of God is simply bursting with excitement. It gives us a glimpse of the mystery and magic that surround each passing day. It reveals to us a world where nothing is simply what it seems but is a coded mystery. When deciphered it speaks to us of the overwhelming presence and awesome beauty of God. It tells us that God is in all things and all things are in God.

Religion should not be seen as merely sanctifying and

safeguarding the status quo. It is always easier to detect the presence and the hand of God in past events but, even if the pattern is not immediately discernible in the present, we can be utterly sure that God is as much in the present and will be in the future as he was in time past. It is only our limited vision that makes us imagine that God created the world once upon a time, in the unimaginable past. He creates here and now; he knows of no past, present, future. Creation is dynamic, constant; it is not static, an event in the past. And all is created in the Word, in God, and reveals something of the infinite reality of God. We do not need to journey far to seek God: in him we live and move and have our being. We simply need to come alive at this moment, and to this moment. As an Eastern mystic said: 'I laugh when I think that the fish in the sea might be thirsty.' To ignore the presence and the reality of God is to live a stunted, maimed life; it is to be blind, deaf and lame in a world of startling beauty.

The message of Christmas is that God's Word has been spoken in flesh and blood, in human terms. But all creation, every event, each human being, all have to be seen as a word of God. All that God has made, is making, will make, is essentially, indivisibly one. Sin divides, disintegrates, destroys. The peace and the happiness and the blessing of Christmas are based on a recognition that all things are one and all created things in their true selves reveal the life and love of God. We can rejoice in that; we are committed to recognising and realising that unity; we must cherish and give birth to God in the present and the future.

The goodwill of the Christmas season is not sentimental benevolence, certainly not merely the expression of the party spirit. It is based on the awareness, confirmed by Christ's birth among us, that God cares constantly, creates endlessly, comes to birth in us and reaches out through us to recognise, welcome, reverence his presence in others and in all things and to remove all bitterness and division.

That is the reality of the present. The future too is not to be feared but welcomed. It will reveal more of human potential, more of the reality of God. All shall be well and all manner of things shall be well.

6:   Epiphany

The substitute celebration of Christmas ends abruptly. Commercially the sales follow hard on the heels of Christmas Day. The Christian festival has served its purpose; it has nothing more to say to the modern world. The genuine celebration of Christmas, however, lingers on because the feast day and all its meaning take time to unfold. It only gradually reveals further tantalising glimpses of a divine mystery which beckons our minds and hearts ever onward and deeper.

Epiphany is the Christmas of the Gentiles – it is a feast of light in the midst of darkness. It commemorates the revealing of the Christ Child to those who were not Jews, to those who came from faraway lands, the Magi who followed the star to Bethlehem. Folk memory calls them kings and says they were three in number. The Gospel of Matthew which tells the story is content to say simply that some wise men came to Jerusalem from the East looking for the newborn king. Their coming to Bethlehem, their gifts to the child of gold, frankincense and myrrh, tell us something more about Christmas and about the God who became man and part of our world and its history.

Epiphany tells us first that the whole world belongs to God and all its peoples are loved by him with equal intensity. The birth of the Messiah is not simply a climax to Jewish history, a fulfilment of the longings and expectations of the Jewish people. The child born of Mary at Bethlehem belongs to the whole of humanity; he has a meaning for every age and all peoples. He more than matched the foretelling of the prophets; he fulfilled every dream of humankind. The coming of the wise men is a sign that God is not a tribal God, can never be identified with national interests. Painful as the realisation may be, we have to recognise that God has no favourites and his mission to the world is to bring light into every darkness, to bring healing wherever there is hurt.

Epiphany reminds us that as brothers and sisters of Christ we are part of a people to be found in every age, to be encountered in every land. This has practical social and political consequences for us. We must be nothing less than Catholic, as we embrace the peoples of every culture and country, and we must be always eager to share the treasure we have in Christ with every living soul. The Church of Christ, and we ourselves, to be true to ourselves, have to be missionary, have to be compulsive communicators of the Good News first heard in the Bethlehem Christmas.

Epiphany teaches us how unchristian and uncatholic it is to be narrow, inward-looking and exclusive. Like the Magi we must be always on pilgrimage, in search of the star, seeking the Christ we can share with others. Epiphany is our mandate to be missionary and concerned about the world outside and all its peoples.

Epiphany reminds us of the wonder of the God made man; we kneel at the crib and ponder the meaning of the gold, frankincense and myrrh brought by the wise men to the newborn king. Christians have always read deep meaning into the gifts. Gold is seen as tribute to a king, frankincense as worshipping a god, myrrh as the burial spices of one who was to be cruelly and decisively rejected. The myrrh is a reminder that the cross already casts its shadow over the crib. Frankincense indicates that ordinary human happenings like birth, death, loving, healing, caring, now take on a new and awesome significance since it is God who is born, dies, loves, heals, cares, is despised and rejected. And gold tells us that the whole human race now has a new hero and king, a leader who would never impose, crush and dominate but who would serve and suffer, inspire and encourage, raise us up to a destiny and a glory beyond all our wildest dreams.

Gold, frankincense and myrrh signify that God becomes both king and willing victim for each of us. Yet he is not a being set apart, not a once-and-for-all messiah. The Christ Child born in Bethlehem is the forerunner of a new humanity to be fashioned in his image. In a sense he is Everyman. Because of him we are each of us to be given the possibility of a new kind of existence, a life like his, bound to him in a unity which is closer than that of flesh and blood. Here we tread on holy ground. What can it mean?

The Son of God, this Jesus born of Mary in Bethlehem, is the revelation of God and the self-giving of God to the human race. He becomes man. Then, by the power of the same Holy Spirit who brought him to be conceived in the Virgin's womb, we, through the signs and symbols of the sacraments, are recreated, born again into a new life, are loved with a new intensity by God. Now God lives in us, takes us to himself, makes us one with himself in Christ, thereby plunging us into the heart of the Godhead. Now we know and are known, love and are loved by the God who has taken us into life and his own love and wants to make us grow into ever deeper unity with his Son through the Holy Spirit. It is a revelation only grasped by faith and in wondering meditation.

Here, understandably, our minds reel and our senses flounder. We grope through darkness which in reality is the intensity of endless light. Here we are at the heart of that supreme mystery which it will be our ecstasy to explore throughout eternity. Christmas and Epiphany are windows into that world. It is the only world worth the winning.

7:   Baptism of the Lord

Most of us live pretty humdrum lives. We rarely rise to the heights. There is precious little to show in our lives for the astonishing love God lavishes on us and for the promises he has made about our destiny and our mission in life. Every time we celebrate Christmas and the cluster of lovely feasts which follow Christmas, including the Epiphany and the Baptism of Our Lord, we are being reminded that the coming of Christ has changed the world for ever. We are not talking about an earth-shattering, super-spectacular act – that is rarely God's way. Instead he seems to favour silence and stealth. He does not cry out or shout aloud, or make his voice heard in the streets. He has transformed all our expectations and changed all our horizons. No longer need we be blinded by ignorance, prejudice or passion – Jesus Christ has come to bring light and truth into the darkness of our minds. No longer do we need to be slaves to our desires, needs, greed, selfishness – Christ shows us that it is possible to live for others and love them, to escape the chains of the weaknesses that imprison. The power of God, the fire of his love, his surging, irresistible life is revealed in Christ, in the babe of Bethlehem and the young carpenter from Nazareth baptised by John in the Jordan. 'This is my beloved Son in whom I am well pleased.'

The promise is that this power, love, life and light can be ours. No one is rejected as worthless or condemned. God does not break the crushed reed, nor quench the wavering flame. No matter what our sins, our failures, there remains the invincible and unwavering love of God for each of us. He will open our blind eyes and free captives from prison, sinfulness and darkness. This is a far cry from the attitude Christians so often display. We doubt our own salvation; we begrudge it to others.

Our failure to believe that this is possible for us, our lack of trust in God's love for us personally, our own laziness and indifference are what stand between us and a new life and energy, a new and deep joy, and a new willingness to forgive others.

Deep down we cannot really accept things as indeed they are. Misled by our childhood experiences, we think we have learned from life that we need to earn love and win approval. We cannot recognise the central revelation of the Gospel that we do not, indeed cannot, earn the favour of God or command his love and approval. Because, independent of all our human qualities or failings, God reveals himself as hopelessly, unconditionally, for ever in love with us. We simply would not exist unless he had not first loved us, shaped the idea of us, expressed himself in us and in all that lives and is. He wants us to love him consciously in return, to recognise that, outside of him, there is literally nothing, and to respond to him in thanksgiving for the love he has lavished on us and all other people and things. We too are parts of a single symphony of beauty and worth. We are baptised as Christ was baptised. What he set out from Nazareth to do we are called to continue in our time through our own lives.

This is a fantastic challenge; it is Christian vocation.

8: Lent

It is a universal and somewhat hackneyed perception that life seems to speed up as one gets older. The years blur into each other. I am constantly surprised by the glimpses I catch of my elderly self in shop windows on the High Street. I wonder where all the years have flown and what there is to show for it. Sometimes and in some moods I wonder if that is all there is to life. Was it worth all the effort? Is that it then?

For those of us slithering downhill and those fortunate enough to have more options open and to be preoccupied with the uphill task of establishing themselves and making something of their lives, the time of Lent each year has a message and a meaning. It is not just about penance and self-denial and the standard practice of giving something up for Lent. It is about liberation, coming alive, learning to live more intensely and more happily. Lent is about life, healing and fulfilment. It challenges us to wake up, open our eyes and dare to live. It is a necessary prelude to Easter and the resurrection which is already now.

Leprosy was a living death. For the people of Christ's day it was like the AIDS epidemic is for us, but even more frightening and more immediately dangerous. Leprosy meant bodily disfigurement, creeping corruption, painful death. It was horrifying to the people of that time precisely because they knew little or nothing about how the disease was caught and how it was spread. They had no cure and no hope. All they could do was to cast out the infected and shun the sick. Leprosy was a disease that disrupted families and destroyed any sense of community. It was feared and loathed. Little wonder, then, that it became a vivid image of sin.

For the people of the past, sickness and sin were seen as somehow interrelated. Both were life-threatening and destructive. Both involved a malfunctioning of the living individual. People had this so deep inside themselves that they found it hard to separate sickness and sin. They imagined that a sick person was sinful or was being punished for sin. But Christ would have none of this. He never regarded the sick and the handicapped as guilty but he certainly saw sickness and sin as part of a creation that had rebelled against God. For him forgiveness of sins and healing the body went hand in hand. In his kingdom, in the new creation, the life-giving energy of God, which we describe as his love, floods into our whole being, restores us to health, physical as well as spiritual, and releases in us our God-given power to live and love. We are made free to forget our fears, insecurity, pettiness and hostility to others. We are liberated from isolation and alienation. We can turn to others and build up community and friendship with them. And we learn to recognise our inner unity and our physical identity as part of God's living and loving creation. It is a fact of Christian experience that it is possible to feel so good and positive that sickness loses its hold on us, that death becomes an irrelevance and no more than a stage in the eternal unfolding of that life of which we are an integral part.

Some who are sick have little or no desire to be well. Sickness can put them centre-stage and give them a claim on others. Sometimes people retreat into sickness to escape what for them is fearful. They retreat from the pressures of living. Some are so obsessed with themselves that they magnify every ache and pain. The hypochondriac is a threatened individual, insecure, afraid to live.

It is necessary first and foremost that we want to be healed and renewed. We have to want to love and live fully, joyously and trustfully. We who are lepers must want a life whole and entire. And that, believe it or not, necessarily means that we want God, for he is source and centre of all life and being.

It is beginning to get a bit clearer now what we are involved in during every Lent. We take ashes at the start of

Lent as recognition and acknowledgement that we are part and parcel of the workaday world which disappoints and disintegrates, which corrupts and is constantly in a process of change. We profess our need for conversion. For most of us that is not a very genuine, personal or urgent priority. Yet conversion is the key that unlocks the new creation and leads us into new existence. We remain, of course, within the same reality which all humans experience but because of a new attitude to life all is transformed. Conversion is a turn-around, a revolution in our attitudes, perceptions and priorities. Christ opened his mission by proclaiming: Repent and believe the Good News. Conversion involves both parts of that process: giving up and giving in. Repentance, on its own, can still be self-centred and self-obsessed. Conversion on the other hand means waking up to the fact that I am not the centre of the universe nor am I the point and purpose of creation. I am totally a gift of God, a word of God, expressing his goodness, love and life. I am made simply to share, rejoice, understand and give thanks. And I am part of an act of love and creation which embraces all ages, the whole human family and all created reality. I die to my limited, pain-ridden, death-threatened, sin-centred isolation.

I shed my leprosy and learn to live a cleansed, transparent, love-filled life that is unending.

So Lent should never be gloomy or negative. Most certainly it is not to be thought of as a boring annual ritual. It is another chance to learn how to wake up and live. There is more to life; it does have hidden secrets. But only the humble, the poor, the little ones, those who live for others will ever learn. We have to be free to die if we want to live.

9: Lent Again

A well-known journalist and television interviewer who described himself as an old-fashioned agnostic, once asked me what quality in people makes them believers. I said I thought it was a certain recklessness, a willingness to take a chance, the daring to take some things on trust. I said I thought a consistently agnostic person would find it hard really to fall in love. If I'd thought of it in time, I would have added that it was also the ability to hope against hope.

It seems to me that it is often the sceptics and materialists who are narrow-minded. They can be pinchpenny, short-sighted and stodgy. Their minds are closed to anything they cannot see, touch, feel, weigh, put a price on. They limit themselves to what they perceive to be rational and evidently verifiable. They are by choice earthbound. Not for them the freedom of the believer who feels at one with God and at peace with others.

The believer sees meaning and purpose in life and in all that is. He or she is undeterred by setbacks, sickness or even death itself. The believer can live every minute to the full – fully alive here and now – for it is only here and now that we experience him. It happens only when we are present to the present. We say of someone lacking good sense: 'they're not all there.' It is an instinctive recognition that to be entirely human involves being all together, in harmony, really here, body, mind and soul.

Buddha was once asked: 'Who is the holy man?' He replied: 'Every hour is divided into a certain number of seconds and every second into a certain number of fractions. He who is able to be totally present in every fraction of a second is indeed a holy man.' A modern writer put the same thought this way: 'The man over whom the future has lost its grip! He resembles the birds of the air and the lilies of the field. No anxieties for tomorrow. Totally in the present. The holy man' (*Song of the Bird*, A. de Melo). The whole person who is both healthy and holy is one for whom the future holds no terrors and the past no regrets. That is certainly holiness but I think it is happiness too. What is more, it is holiness and happiness within the grasp of each of us. Lent, if we let it, will show us how.

The prophets of old and Isaiah in particular painted pictures of liberation, renewal and peaceful possession that even today make us catch our breath at their beauty. Christ undoubtedly saw himself as the fulfilment of prophecy and as the living answer to the prayers and longings of an expectant people. He embodies God's faithfulness, his willingness to heal and forgive. The Gospel tells us of that dramatic moment when Christ snatched from certain death the woman caught in the act of adultery. Here we see redeeming and reconciling love in action. He does not condone her sin – but does not condemn and shows her instead how to live again. He encourages her to put away wickedness, turn to goodness, live a new life to the full and learn a new kind of love. To realise what that means in practice we have to ponder what it means to be part of renewed and risen humanity. We are no longer a fallen but a redeemed people. St Paul was insistent in his teaching: 'All I want is to know Christ and the power of his resurrection and to share his sufferings by reproducing the pattern of his death ... All I can say is that I forget the past and I strain ahead for what is still to come' (Phil. 3:11–14).

Like the sinful woman and the wayward Jews, we are not just offered in our lives a second chance but a life of endless chances. Every moment is a moment of grace when we can encounter here and now the God who is. The individual who is all there, who lives the radical, transformed life of constant conversion realises that what the Gospel means by conversion is not constant regrets, zigzagging from bad to good and back again, but coming to accept that the secret of unending, here-and-now happiness is to be alive and present to God. In prayer, awareness, rapt attention, we focus on the beauty, infinity and timelessness of God. In this experience there is truly no past, no future, only the eternal now. Here all reality is experienced in an unending moment of ever-present ecstasy.

These are no better than threadbare words. All too often, rather than be alone with the God who is, we step back, refuse to pay attention and be present. We prefer appearances, the surface of things. We seek out the secondhand; we escape from the awfulness of silence and self by the noise in our ears, the changing scene, each passing fancy. Lent each year is a time to refocus on the face of Christ and to see the God-light in him. Was there ever such beauty in a son of man? It is the time to listen to his voice: has any man spoken as he did? It is the time to feel the magic of his love: has anyone loved this world as he did, the sinless who became sin that we might be the goodness of God?

Every year Lent reminds us that we need never lose hope because the God who is revealed to us is not a distant, dispassionate God. God is here in the darkness, despair and loneliness. He is here when defeat and death stare us in the face. We live in a brutal, violent world but it is a world whose wickedness is already forgiven, because Christ in his love died for us. Since then the torn fabric of our world is being gradually 'rewoven'. We live in a world where the sun shines for us without ceasing provided we are willing in faith and hope. We slowly are brought to live in that unending and uniquely creative present, locked into the love of God, committed without limit to the love of others.

That is a glimpse of what is meant by repentance, conversion and prayer. It is the heart of every Lent.

10:   The Sacred Three Days

Face to face with the passion of Jesus Christ we have to stand and stare, to tremble at both the memory and the present reality of the God who takes to himself all human pain and fear and the agony of death. Once again we are taken into the heart of life's mystery: what it means to suffer; why our life is beset by danger, defeat and despair. All we know for certain is that God is at the heart of it, that God finds his way to the fulfilment of all things along the road of sorrows, mankind's *via dolorosa.*

We listen attentively to the retelling of the ancient story, to what happened at one distant Passover time in the city of Jerusalem to a man named Jesus. It is a sad but familiar story that perhaps has lost its power to stun and amaze. I rarely fail to marvel at the enormity of what we say so glibly we believe as Christians. That this man Jesus was none other than the living power and presence of the Almighty. In this man, God, who is the sole source and inner reality of all that exists, chose to become man, to live, love, heal and then be put to a cruel death. If anything of this is true it is the one supremely significant fact of all history. It gives new meaning and point to being human, to all my living and my experience of suffering and death. If any of this is true then I am already made whole, free, singled out for a destiny of endless fulfilment and love.

The three days of intense prayer and worship which we call the Easter Triduum form a single, unique unity from beginning to end. It begins on Maundy Thursday, when in sign and symbol we become part of Christ's Last Supper with his disciples. We make our own his practical, humble love. The washing of the apostles' feet shames us into our own individual ministry of service, caring and compassion. We are inspired to share his longing love for the Father and for the world for which he laid down his life. His eucharist, his total giving becomes increasingly our own.

On Good Friday we are sacramentally part of his mortal struggle with the power of death, the forces of darkness and evil. On Calvary Jesus took on himself the brokenness and the despair of all humanity, looked into the abyss of fear and still loved in absolute obedience and without compromise or flinching. In him love conquered hatred; life overcame death. We are being shown how to face all that life can bring and how to find fulfilment.

At the Easter Vigil we are caught up in the glory and triumph of Easter. In darkness and defeat, the empty tomb and the fleeting appearances of the risen Christ are enough to convince the believer that here is the final victory. Christ has risen from the dead and because of that, the whole human race is assured of unending life and a destiny that can only stun and amaze. We are talking here about everyday life, about here and now, and not just about the life of our souls or life after death. When we talk about new life, real hope, we are talking about today and a new experience we can all share. We are talking about every aspect of life, both that part which we instinctively recognise as spiritual and sacred, as well as the equally sacred which we describe as secular.

Christ's Easter rising is our human history; it reveals the inner energy and secret of our world. When the world suffers, God is at the heart of that suffering; he has a plan and purpose for us that we can only guess at. In and through us God loves his creation and leads it to its fulfilment in ways that demand our utter trust and complete acceptance. In his rising he affirms that all shall be well and all manner of things shall be well. The ongoing story of the human family vindicates that faith.

It is easy to say that and then lock it away in the back of our minds, ignoring it in the daily business of our lives. We behave and react as if death is still the supreme tragedy. We think of ourselves as sinful, guilty and essentially part of fallen humanity as if Jesus Christ has not already won forgiveness for our sins.

The message of Easter is simple to summarise but endlessly rich and reassuring. A man like us went to his death without wavering in his trust in God his Father, in absolute innocence, in total love. In the truest sense, Jesus Christ was another Adam, another representative and symbol of our human race. In Adam all sin and are doomed to die; in Christ, all who believe are reconciled and are destined to glory. We are all, through baptism, made a new people, Christ's people. The Old Testament is a closed book; the former covenant is transformed into the new alliance. We live now as children, sons and daughters of God; we are in a real, literal sense, people of the new covenant. Easter says we have already faced and defeated death. Christ did it for us; we do it now with him. Now we live a new kind of life, a risen life given us first in baptism, built up by communion and all the sacraments which are signs and symbols that make real what they signify.

Our life in Christ is to be sealed and made glorious when we receive the last sacrament and encounter God for the final ecstatic, endless time when we physically die and enter fully into the eternal life which is first made ours in baptism. Here and now, we should not talk and act as if we are still sinners, a fallen race. We are Christ's people and the communion of saints risen from sin and selfishness. We are not marked out any longer for death and oblivion. We should be living in the sunlight of God's life and love; we can, and should, be renewing the face of the earth, gradually and consciously throughout each day of our lives becoming an Easter people. Religion is about becoming real, whole, belonging to God and endlessly alive.

Easter tells us that this is our life and our calling. In the Easter mystery God commits himself to every one of us, to the whole human race and says in very truth: 'I am with you to the end of time. My life and love are yours for the asking. Come to me in faith, die to your selfish narrowness, live now and for ever in freedom, love and boundless life.'

For all that we do, our inventions, technology, work, relationships and the society we build, are all done in Christ whether we are conscious of it or not. As believers we should indeed be increasingly conscious that God is in all things and all things are in God. He is the everlasting and inexhaustible spring of life and love that is constantly welling up into our world and constantly renewing its vitality. Easter is a sign and cause of this.

11: Good Friday

Nothing much seems to change. TV, radio and newspapers bring each day news of mindless pain needlessly inflicted. In Africa there is the slow death of chronic malnutrition and starvation. In the Middle East there is blind hatred and fanaticism. In South Africa familiar but still sickening brutality of police repression and violence and the increasing conflict between black factions. In Northern Ireland there is sporadic but ruthless terrorism and political response which is predictable and so often unintelligent. At home we experience much cruelty, abuse of children, urban ugliness and hooliganism. There remains for many the grinding despair of long-term unemployment and the sense of uselessness. We encounter in our own lives the sadness of bereavement, the trials of sickness and physical and mental handicap, tensions, anxieties, depression, the daily string of misunderstandings, betrayals and conflicts which cloud our happiness. Without being morbid or obsessed, it would seem that for a lot of people, most of the time, every day is a lot like Good Friday. We used to call the world in our devotions of yesteryear – 'the vale of tears'. And many people still turn to us with fear and distress in their eyes and say: Where is God in all this? Is life a cruel deception? What is the use of telling us about a loving God, a Jesus who saves? Where is the so-called Good News you say Christ brought to the world? Is religion a failure and a hoax?

We cannot duck these questions, especially as we live out in our Christian lives the reality of Holy Week and Good Friday. We are reminded yet again of the pain, the scourging, the public humiliation and the shameful execution of Jesus

Christ. But is the Calvary of Christ anything out of the ordinary? Is it not just another example of how idealism, love and promise fall foul of human sin and official blindness? Does Good Friday change history in any way?

Certainly pain and suffering remain. Obviously Jesus Christ and those who follow him can never claim to end the sequence of bitter pain. The world is on the rack. There will never be on this planet an earthly paradise of unending and universal peace, plenty and ease. How then to make sense of suffering? How to understand pain? How to learn to live with and through it? How to grow in human stature and dignity through it?

We struggle and fail to find the answers in philosophy, or human reckoning. We have been told that God's foolishness outstrips human wisdom. The way forward can only be to look to the cross, ponder its significance, read and reread the accounts of Christ's passion and death. The first two chapters of St Paul's first letter to the Corinthians contain the 'secret and hidden wisdom of God'. If we pray through this we will begin to perceive the glimmer of meaning: the scandal of the cross, the foolishness of God's fond love for us, the overturning of all our human categories of assessment. The human family is committed to a journey through time that, because of its challenge and difficulty, painfully, step by step, leads to greater understanding and the release of the divine potential within our human nature.

It helps me, as well, to picture Jesus Christ as Everyman. He took on himself the life, the laughter, the loving, sickness and sin of our human existence. He became not just our figurehead but, in a sense, our very selves. We are used to thinking of Christians as united with Christ, forming his body, being his people. In a real sense, though, he is us, he is me. When I read of the daily events, the simplicity, fellowship, prayers, healing, suffering, death and glory of his life, I can say that this is my experience too. As Christ experiences and lives through this, so do I. He gives new meaning and purpose to my limited life, he lifts it up to a level where Godhead and humanity meet and become one. In Christ the whole human family suffers; in suffering humanity, Christ continues his passion and his sacrifice until the end of time.

This world, this brief and often bleak existence, is not the beginning nor the end of any of us nor of the human story. The words of the hymn take on a special truth. *I was there when they crucified my Lord.* For there is another dimension; a world behind and within this world; a life and an energy that penetrate and animate this material universe. We can so easily lose sight of this inner mystery. The only way to rediscover the secret of existence is to seek out the source of all things, to search for God, to find that he is a doting Father and to realise that we too are son or daughter. Like Christ we must be prepared to do his will in humble service, to love without why or wherefore and to find that in being prepared to die we are free to live. If we are ready to die in every detail, if we learn to prize love and righteousness above everything else, then gradually we learn how to live and how to die and how to discover the path to fulfilment. How do we know? How can we be sure? We look to Everyman. We look to Christ who like Moses has led us out of slavery and death. We look at the cross and see behind the cross the features of the risen Christ.

This is the decisive way forward and a comprehensive programme for life. To make sense of daily problems and to grow as genuine human beings, we have to be ready to accept this mysterious contradiction as true in every aspect of life: we can never live unless we are prepared to die. We have to be free to see the positive aspects of any situation. We can never truly enjoy anything unless we feel ourselves free to deny ourselves pleasure. We can never be free unless we are prepared to recognise and respond to the claims of God and of our neighbour. We have to learn that self-denial somehow makes us appreciate for the first time the true beauty and worth of things.

That is the secret of Lent and of every Good Friday. It is the wisdom of ages brought to us by Christ and his Church. Most of us never make it part of our thinking. We remain in daily life children of this world, selfish, self-centred and enslaved. And yet all the time we are being beckoned forward into freedom by Jesus himself. We have for too long been preoccupied or frightened to understand and respond. If we really grasp that Christ, as the Word, is the inmost reality of all things, how can we be blind to the truth that death and resurrection constitute the fundamental biorhythm of creation?

12: Easter

I walked through the park one Sunday astonished by the suddenness of spring. After the darkness and uncertainty of the short winter days there are spring flowers and the stirrings of life. We glory in that life; we rejoice in the celebration of the Easter liberation. We give thanks for the gift of life and love.

Throughout every Lent I have to keep reminding myself that it is not about denial and deprivation but about the discipline of learning to live. It is about coming alive to the richness and the magic of existence. I have learned to savour with real understanding those miraculous words of Paul: 'We are God's work of art, created in Christ Jesus to live the good life as from the beginning he had meant us to live it' (Eph. 2:10). Here there is a truth that can transform. It is a far cry from the dreary and incessant put-down of our humanity that formed the constant refrain of preaching and teaching when I was young. I suspect it was then as much a cultural as a religious imperative to be niggardly with praise and affirmation. There was a heartfelt enthusiasm behind all the efforts to cut us down to size, to stop us getting ideas about ourselves.

But the Word of God says boldly: 'We are God's work of art'. We are his masterpiece – body and soul. We are not a hopeless reject but the ultimate beauty. In our dreaming, striving, loving and living we never cease to reflect the beauty of God's Word in whose image and likeness we are all fashioned and made. In the depths and reality of our own human nature we encounter God, can speak with him face to face as friend speaks to friend. We ought not to seek God primarily out there and up there but rather in the heart of our own being. Our principal and constant quest for God leads us into our inmost selves, into the silent centre of our being where God dwells. There he is to be discovered in silence, emptiness and rapt attentiveness. In our thirst for life we return to the spring which is within our very selves. That is where there is goodness and life and unceasing hope, not alienation, ugliness and death.

And the purpose of our existence: 'We are created in Christ Jesus to live the good life as from the beginning he had meant us to live it'. Here is a bold assertion, positive and healing. There is no hint here of timidity, of withdrawal from life and activity, of guilt and inhibition. God's creation in all its physical and actual reality is a revelation of goodness and love, not a minefield of temptation and distraction, and certainly not a fearful, guilt-ridden interlude before our eternal, disembodied, heavenly reward. God's plan, from Genesis to his ultimate revelation in Christ, is to share with all creation his life and love. We are part of the process of his creation; we are made to share in it and to shape it by our faithful living of the good life, natural and fully human. It is a vast relief and an enormous encouragement to know that daily life and our human relationships are not an irrelevance, not a passing and doomed delight, but the very stuff of eternity.

Is there then no sin, no distortion? From whence springs frustration and disillusion? Human history and our own experience witness to folly and dislocation. That is when we make ourselves the focus, the insistent and intrusive centre of our world. Then we fragment the unity of God's world. We hijack what is meant for all in pursuit of our selfish and shortsighted ends. No matter how crass and selfish we are, we can never utterly destroy God's masterpiece, his work of art. The beauty remains under the layers of grime and the reworking of lesser artists. Our Christian endeavour is really to let the divine craftsman and restorer peel off the layers of irrelevance to reveal the original beauty beneath.

That is part of our every Lent: to rediscover the good life, to allow God's goodness to shine through our weakness and to become fully human. Then we learn to live as Easter people in the sunshine of God's love.

13: After Easter

We ought to probe a bit deeper into real life, to think about the things we were often too busy or too lazy to reflect on. When were are young we were sometimes bewildered by the choices before us; when we grow older, we can feel bitter at the way life has turned out. We may sense we have lost our way; we may regret perhaps the choices we in fact made; we can get frustrated with our diminished opportunities, our failure to be effective. Common to us all is the feeling that we need to know where we are going, our purpose in life. We need to feel that we have something worth living for, something that in its turn gives us a sense of being worthwhile people living significant lives. We need to feel that we can change and that other people and things too can be changed. We need a faith, a hope, a star to guide us on our way.

This is more difficult than we generally realise. We are living in a world which is changing at a dizzying pace. In this country we experience the collective tiredness and fragmentation which goes with the collapse of a once-mighty empire and the ageing of a people with a long and energetic history. In the Western world we are in the midst of a crisis of commitment. In Europe we have, as a continent, thrown aside our inherited Christian values and standards. We seek a new identity. Society has lost its cohesion and its confidence. *La peste blanche*, as a French writer calls it – 'the white plague' – is sapping our will to live, our joy in loving. Surveys on European values reveal a prevailing sense of boredom, of flatness. There appears to be nothing worth living or fighting for. Is it any wonder that our society is riddled with treachery and our relationships with deceit and unfaithfulness? On top of that, our industrial shake-up has resulted in widespread unemployment and social confusion and insecurity. This is not just economically dangerous in the long term but psychologically threatening here and now as we rob human beings not just of their jobs but of their sense of identity and worth.

The wisdom of God calls us to reflect on this unused potential which is both individual and collective. The perpetual coming of Christ and the kingdom of God on earth rejects decisively the notion that *there is no alternative*. We are called to step firmly out of the swirling mists of confusion and moral bankruptcy. There is an alternative to all this. There is a faith to live by, a hope to long for. There is purpose and meaning in life. There are values that are valid and will secure a worthwhile world where people can be content, can flourish, can maintain their dignity and find their fulfilment.

But we cannot look solely to the stock exchange for salvation, or to market forces, the boardroom and the banks for abundance of life. We must not look to political parties, the constitution and the legal system for justice and fair dealing. We will not find peace and security through missile systems or the military. These have their role, but they, like the pharaohs and the emperors of old, will all one day crumble to dust. We need a surer foundation. We need an unfailing spring of living water. Like the wise men from the East we should follow the star that leads to a stable. We have to rid ourselves of our illusions, shed our pomp and self-importance and bend down humbly to embrace the king who appears and is so pitifully puny, powerless and poor. He has nothing but is everything. He will be hounded by the powerful from the day of his birth to the hour of his crucifixion. But he alone can lead us sure-footed through life, into the very jaws of death and through to the land of eternal promise.

When we have found our Christ and when we have found ourselves in finding him, then we must offer his hope to a world which does not know what it wants but knows there must be something better than what it has. That does not mean that we should scold the world or bewail it. We must go to people and say: 'Don't let's waste all this untapped potential; let's find together something that's worth living for and working for; let's build as best we can a better world, a society with a human face, where human values and relationships are cherished and upheld.' But first there must be a kind of death.

14: Pentecost

Pentecost exercises a special kind of fascination. It summons up so many of the images and ideas which now sustain me. Pentecost Sunday is the birthday of the whole Church. The coming of the Holy Spirit in fire and mighty wind represents the glory of God, a momentous act of creation, the reshaping of our humanity. In the opening chapters of Genesis the Spirit of God broods over the waters and chaos; the earth and all its living things are brought forth. At Pentecost we tread the path of poetry, symbol and mystery. We are being led into the fullness of truth. Creation and Pentecost are both supreme acts of God; both are a sharing in his life and love. Creation is a coming out from God in diversity; Pentecost the beginning of a conscious healing and reconciliation in which all things are gradually being brought back to the original unity.

Scientists with some justice now claim to be able to analyse the first milliseconds of the Big Bang which shaped the 18 billion years of cosmic history. In 1965 they discovered the echoes of that first explosion; it was a persistent radio-active whisper picked up from every part of the sky. It was like listening in to God's act of creation. I find that extraordinarily moving. Analogously, it enables me to picture Pentecost as the spiritual Big Bang whose effects still shape our history, whose echoes still reverberate throughout the cosmos and whose whisper can be heard on every side if we are tuned in to listen.

Creation is not a far-off, once-and-for-all event. God did not light the blue touch-paper, stand back, and let the rocket soar. Creation is, creation continues, creation is perpetual. Far from being up there and out there, God is at the heart of all that is; he is best imaged as the inmost heart of all that is. He is everything in everything, one God, maker and Father of all. Yet we compress 18 billion years of creation into the bare phrase of the Creed: creator of heaven and earth. The endless diversity of all that exists is in reality the single pulse of divine energy.

Just as creation is perpetual, we have to come to understand in the depths of ourselves that Pentecost too is perpetual, happens now and will never cease to happen. This insight given to the West from the East explains something that always vaguely disturbed me. Why is the return of the Lord so long in coming? Early disciples lived in anticipation of the Last Day. Since then we have had to get used to indefinite postponement. Christians, like the disciples, stood on their Tabor, scanning the skies, searching for their departed Christ, desperately longing for his return in glory, for the second coming of the Prince of life, of love, of peace. As a result of centuries of Christian pessimism many of us still picture ourselves in the vale of tears, living in a fallen world among the fallen, as exiles dreaming of a home beyond the skies, all our hope focussed on a world beyond this world, a time beyond this time. What has been staring us in the face for two millennia is that the coming has not been postponed indefinitely nor has Christ now departed this life to be in paradise. God has been faithful to his promise. The covenant is in place. Christ is among us and can never be separated from the reality that is being constantly fashioned in his likeness. Pentecost itself can be seen in the deepest sense as the second coming; the decisive re-entry, if you like, of the Spirit of Christ, the power of the Holy Spirit, taking possession of a world that can never be alien to God. The hearts and minds of God's children through the Holy Spirit become alive to God, welcome him, seek union and fulfilment with him, make him present in the here and now. At the Annunciation and in Bethlehem's stable, God became man in Jesus, the first fruits of the new creation. At Pentecost, through faith, all humanity was seized by the Spirit to become a single cosmic Christ, a new creation in a new age.

For all time, henceforth, now and for ever, humankind and, through humanity, all that exists – on this planet and in the cosmos – can live and share the one life, the one love. We, the scattered, the diverse, are drawn back to the unity that exists for ever, and is endless love. Christ, to the end of time, brings all of us, and all creation, into the throbbing heart of the Triune God, Father, Son and Holy Spirit.

It has taken the human race many millennia to realise the true shape of the world. The images of our planet reproduced in an incredible book, *The Home Planet*, were unthinkable a mere 30 years ago. As we begin hesitantly to explore the universe we are slowly accepting the unity of our planet, the reality of our history, its place in the universe, its origin and likely fate. It is hard for us to be aware that our planet is circling the sun at 62,000 miles an hour and spins on its axis at 1,000 miles an hour. The sun which is the centre of our solar system moves around our galaxy at more than 500,000 miles an hour. The galaxy itself moves at unimaginable speeds through a universe populated with billions of other galaxies. And yet we imagine our earth to be solid, stable, the very centre of all that matters!

In the past there have been tensions and contradictions between science and religion. It was a conflict which disfigured the centuries of the Renaissance, the Enlightenment, the age of Newton, Darwin and Einstein. Now in our age the true believer is called as never before to embrace all knowledge as a revealing of the mind of God. After two millennia Christians now are beginning to realise and rejoice in the heights and the depths, the breadth and extent of our new creation and our place in God's glory. Pentecost – like Genesis – plunges us into the heart of mystery, wonder and joyful thanksgiving.

God was born into our world in Bethlehem 2,000 years ago. He continues to be born into our humanity whenever the Spirit is welcomed: Be it done unto me according to thy word. Christ, the cosmic Christ, the sacrament of all humankind, is here among us as the Church. Christ, incarnate Word, is growing to maturity, until he becomes truly all in all. That is what gives meaning and purpose to all intervening history and to the future. In this new age, the new covenant, the living reality of God continues to take hold of humanity, reshaping reality and preparing the human family for an unimaginable future.

We need a radical shift in our perception of God if we are to adjust our vision to the new creation in which we live. God is eternal; our understanding of him is finite and fallible. I am moved by the words of David Jones: 'It is easy to miss him at the turn of a civilisation.' All the pictures of God we have in our heads, all our ideas about ourselves and our relationship with him have to take account of the flood of knowledge, discovery and research that is shaping – for our generation uniquely – a new and stunning awareness of creation and our place in it. Forty years ago Fred Hoyle the astronomer said: 'Once a photograph of the earth taken from the outside is available, a new idea as powerful as any in history will be let loose.' Now that these photographs are freely available they make us aware of the unity of our world and its peoples and the need for utterly committed stewardship of our fragile planet. That makes nonsense of many of our human ambitions and deadly rivalries in the past. How could we have lived, for example, with a divided and nationalistic Europe, with the deadly rivalries of the Middle East, with a world at war, with fragmentation and brokenness? It is an indictment of the world we have created that there is only one year this century, 1968, when a British soldier did not die in action. And this after 2,000 years of Christian endeavour for the coming of God's kingdom.

I think we have to allow some of the Gospel images of the kingdom used by Jesus to grow within a new cosmic context. Jesus described the kingdom as mustard seed, leaven and light. They are images which imply growth, transformation, energy and understanding. Here is nothing static, predictable, alien or otherworldly.

The coming of the kingdom, that perpetual Pentecost which makes real the presence of Christ in our world, should manifest these three things – growth, transformation, understanding. All are possible because God, the innermost energy source of all creation, became man and wants to become the inner reality of the whole of humanity. He is making humankind the channel of his life, intelligence, energy and order in the whole universe.

The Christian faith and spirituality are now more relevant and significant than ever. The coming of the God-man into our human family 2,000 years ago sets the seal on God's plan for the evolution of his creation. It releases divine life and love into humanity; it makes it possible for the human mind to glimpse the pattern and plan behind creation.

The images of the kingdom remind us that the presence of Christ in us and in our world spells growth and life. The kingdom will eventually embrace the whole of creation. Yet it is never something alien imposed from without. It is inherent and connatural. It springs from within and is inexhaustible. All that is needed for its growth is an awakening to the truth and a turning to the light.

It also means transformation, the leavening of matter which modern science sees to be not inert but possessing its own ceaseless dance of inner energy. The human mind is capable of observing, analysing and redirecting the potential of the cosmos. We are made in the image and likeness of the God who creates and we too are called to share his endless creativity. Yet in all this we must collaborate, not exploit. We are stardust like all that exists in our universe. Uniquely we are spirit and in a special way reflect God in whose image and likeness we are made, but we are also, as Thomas Berry says, cousins of all creation. I read recently something by Jane Blewitt: 'In the Big Bang (or more accurately the Great Light) was contained all that is in the universe, all that has unfolded eon upon eon, galaxies, solar systems, our earth, life, right down to the present moment. From the first, every particle carried within it the seeds of the next unfolding, including human consciousness.' That sets in a new context the process of creation and its unity.

The coming of Christ and, in particular, the advent of his Spirit, 'the great light', gives us understanding and light. It is becoming clear that the mission of the human family, gripped by a vision, is to go out to a seemingly barren universe and into lifeless galaxies and make them flower into new and purposeful life. Coming as we do from the outer rim of the cosmos – a cosmic Bethlehem – humanity, given unity, life and love in Christ, will yet make God's kingdom come throughout all his creation and bring creative light into the darkness, the friendly darkness that has reigned there from the beginning.

Those are the far horizons. Under our feet, at our own doorstep, there is a danger that we can destroy our environment, poison our planet, be dealers of death. Fine talk of destiny and glory ignores the deadly reality of our own sin. In our spirituality we have to remain conscious of the possibility of failure without being crippled by unending guilt. I find it helps me to make sense of our human condition by recalling the strange contorted responses so many politicians in the West made at the end of the 1980s to the Soviet peace campaign and the ending of the Cold War. An American former arms control expert talking on TV after Gorbachev's offer at the United Nations of unilateral disarmament said: 'The trouble with Caspar Weinberger and those who think like him is that they need an enemy, are only happy when they can identify an enemy, lose the shape of their world if the enemy no longer exists.' What struck me at the time was that this formulated a profound truth, valid not only for Cold War warriors but for many of us so much of the time and indeed central to many people's sense of their own identity. We define ourselves as much by what we hate and fear as by what we love and stand for.

It does seem that we have a compulsion within ourselves to express in attitudes and actions the profound alienation within our inmost selves which is the consequence of sin. The medieval mystic Meister Eckhart taught that the sin behind all sin is dualism, the constant perception of a divide between us and them, between me and the rest, between the sacred and the secular, the safe and the dangerous. Peace and human progress are impossible unless we face up to and overcome this inner division, the need for an enemy.

The difficulty and complexity of confronting this deeply rooted, deeply felt attitude should not be minimised. Many of our accepted and often unquestioned religious responses, a lot, too, of our spiritual activity, are based on the recognition of enemies: the world, or Catholics, or Protestants, or Jews, or Freemasons, or ethnic minorities, or even, God help us, our own selves. Much of our religious thinking and many of our moral responses are based upon concepts of warfare, antagonism, self-disgust and rejection. Some Christians, even now, cannot fully accept the body as sacred to the indwelling God, nor the universe which gives birth to our human reality, nourishes and loves it, nor find a place in their spirituality for the richness of all that exists. Theirs is still the response of barely concealed abhorrence.

I am reminded of the story of the Welshman shipwrecked on a desert island. When he was rescued, it was noticed that he had built two structures on his island. When he was asked to explain he said: 'That's easy. One was the chapel I went to. The other was the church I wouldn't be seen dead in.' The Christian believer has all too often been taught to hate, to divide, to dominate.

The real message of the Gospel is not so much that we should love our enemies but in reality – in God's reality – we have no enemy. Just as God has no enemy. He can't stop loving – even the damned, the fallen angels and Lucifer himself. He is only opposed to the nothingness which is non-God. That is the blankness, the nihilism of sin. In all that he creates he can see only the reflection of himself, the Word in whom all things are made. And that he loves endlessly, unconditionally.

He persists in the perpetual process of bringing back into unity what he has created as a symphony of love, a single outpouring of unending beauty, goodness and truth. Underneath all the diversity and the apparently irreconcilable is the single reality, the infinitude of God, the unity that has to be eventually realised so that God may be all in all. Spirituality is best thought of not in terms of warfare but as a matter of harmony, reconciliation, interdependence.

The mind and heart given to God, dead to selfishness and alienation, by that very commitment have to be alive and sensitive to all that exists, loving self and others in the same movement of the Spirit. We do not arrive at this state of mind primarily as a result of moral discipline and self-denial, although, properly understood, they have a vital part to play in helping us to focus and to stay faithful to our vision. Instead we have to begin by trying to grasp the whole picture, the spiritual cosmos of which we are an integral and endlessly loved part. It is essential to be real, to be part of reality and to take that reality seriously and with absolute reverence.

There is something deeply sacred about the whole of creation. The sacred book of the universe joins the sacred book of the Scriptures as privileged places where the Word of God is to be found, where the revelation of God is made. We have to read and ponder both books, stretching out to understand, make them our own, make them one in our minds and in our hearts. So we must dwell on the Word of God in scripture and creation, pondering both in our hearts. That leads to response, a constant act of thanksgiving, of eucharist. It is the basic prayer response of the created, of those called out of nothingness, summoned blinking into the light. And then there erupts praise, the expression of wonder and awe at the marvels of God. Prayer is the state of realisation in which we consciously become what we already truly are. It is not at all the recitation of prayer words but a constant awareness of ourselves as centred on God. We, in prayer, find in our inmost depths the still pool of being where we share God's very life and his love. It becomes a prayer without words, without images. Instead we stay silent and still at the very core of our existence. Here we find, day by day, the secret of lasting inner peace which is far removed from self-satisfaction, complacency or freedom from threat. We pierce the cloud of unknowing to find in the depths of our inner selves the peace which is absolute, unending because founded in God and our unbroken unity with him. It is a peace which lies beneath the occasional storms of self, of personal assertiveness, of opposition and rejection. It is free from fear of others, of our own darkness, and from any fear of death. It is an entry into a state where we are content to let the power and life of God manifest itself in us. It is far from passivity and blandness. It is the unleashing of ceaseless energy. We become a conscious part of the Great Light, part of the perpetual coming of the kingdom of God. We become other Christs.